José Fernande
Przemysław Sku

Colour illustrations by
Teodor Liviu Moroșanu

# Douglas F3D
# SKYKNIGHT

STRATUS

STRATUS s.c.
Po. Box 123,
27-600 Sandomierz 1, Poland
e-mail: office@mmpbooks.biz
for
Mushroom Model Publications,
3 Gloucester Close, Petersfield,
Hampshire GU32 3AX, UK.
E-mail: rogerw@mmpbooks.biz
© 2014 MMPBooks.
http://www.mmpbooks.biz

**ISBN**

**978-83-61421-70-2**

*Editor in chief*
**Roger Wallsgrove**

*Editorial Team*
**Bartłomiej Belcarz
Artur Juszczak
James Kightly
Robert Pęczkowski**

*DTP*
**Stratus s.c**

*Text:*
**José Fernandez
Przemysław Skulski
Paul Eden**

*Colour Drawings*
**Teodor Liviu Moroşanu**

*Scale Plans*
**Dariusz Karnas**

*Printed by:*
*Drukarnia Diecezjalna,
ul. Żeromskiego 4,
27-600 Sandomierz*
PRINTED IN POLAND

# Table of contents

*Title page: Douglas F-10B Skyknight (F3D-2), 124598/4598. (Richard Dann Collection via J. Fernandez)*

# Introduction

The Douglas F3D Skyknight, nicknamed "Willie the Whale", was the first purpose-designed and -built jet night fighter. It saw the service with both the United States Navy and the United States Marine Corps for a surprisingly long time and was the only jet combat aircraft to take part in both the Korean and Vietnam Wars. During the Korean War Skyknights scored several victories as a night fighter. During the Vietnam conflict the role was different – the F3D served as an electronic warfare platform.

*F3D Skyknight with markings of VMF(N)-513 on display on the deck of USS* Intrepid *Museum, New York. (B. Belcarz)*

# Birth and Development

In August 1945, the American Bureau of Aeronautics issued a requirement for a shipboard night fighter. The specification called for an all-weather fighter having a maximum speed of 500mph (800 km/h) capable of reaching an altitude of 40,000 ft (12,300 metres) and of detecting an enemy aircraft within a radius of 125 miles (200 km).

The complexity of the radar necessary to fulfil this task called for a second crew member. The radar requirement was exceptional for the time, calling for the incorporation of a very large radar disc. The Westinghouse APQ-35 radar, then under development, was selected and sufficient place had to be allowed for it when it was finally ready for service.

Four manufacturers, Douglas, Curtiss, Grumman and Fleetwing, replied to the request for this night fighter.

*The rear view of the second prototype of the XF3D-1 (BuNo 121458). (US National Archives)*

The Douglas proposition was accepted on 3 April 1946 and confirmed by an order for three prototypes under the designation XF3D-1 Skyknight. Under the direction of Ed Heinemann, a team of engineers and technicians at the Douglas plant at El Segundo (California) began work on the first prototype. On completion, the first XF3D-1 was moved to Edwards Air Force Base at Muroc Dry Lake, where its bulbous shape led to its nickname – "Willy the Whale".

Test pilot Russell Thaw flew the first prototype on 23 March 1948. The second prototype XF3D-1 flew on 6 June 1948 and the third on 7 October of the same year. Flight tests continued without any problems and a contract for production of an initial series of 28 F3D-1 was signed on 11 May 1948. The main difference between the XF3D-1 and the F3D-1 was in the type of Westinghouse engine installed – the prototypes were fitted with the J-34-WE-22 having a thrust of 3,000 lb (1,360 kg) and the initial series with the more powerful J-34-WE-38 (3,250 lb/1,472 kg thrust).

While they were still at Muroc, the US Air Force also tested the XF3D and, as a result, fitting afterburners was considered in order to meet USAF specifications. However, it was decided to stick with the F-94 Starfire, a development of the T-33, this being provisionally adopted until the F-89 Scorpion became available.

The size of the radar disc called for the adoption of a very large nose. Also, the configuration of the cockpit with two crew side by side and the incorporation of four 20 mm cannon made for a very large forward fuselage, but the after part was of classic form and quite similar to the Skyraider. The engines were incorporated into the fuselage under the wing roots. The fuel tanks were also situated within the fuselage above the engines. The tricycle landing gear was supplemented by a tail wheel as a precaution against damage during rough landings.

*F3D-1 of VFM(N)-542 in flight over El Toro (California) in 1951. (US National Archives)*

*An F3D-2 (BuNo 124634) at the Douglas Aircraft Factory, 1953. In front of the aircraft, Ed Heinemann, Douglas engineer, receives the keys for a new Oldsmobile Super 88 De Luxe car. (US National Archives)*

*F3D-2M (BuNo 125882) "882" during a stay at the Naval Air Missile Center, Point Mugu, April 1961. (Richard Dann Collection via J. Fernandez)*

The Skyknight's crew escape system was a unique feature. Exit from above the cockpit ran the risk of injury and the provision of ejection seats proved to be a penalty in terms of cost and weight. The system devised for in-flight evacuation involved tilting the crew's seats rearwards and sliding them downward and out below the aircraft to the rear. Having left the aircraft, the crew were to wait for five seconds before pulling the ripcords of their parachutes so as to avoid any risk of entanglement with the aircraft.

Meanwhile, in October 1948, the Naval Air Test Center (NATC) at Patuxent River in Maryland and the MCAS at El Toro carried out simulated night interception tests. The results obtained were highly satisfactory, with single-engined jet aircraft being intercepted and destroyed at altitudes above 39,000 ft (12,000 metres).

The first two prototypes were fitted with the SCR720 radar. However this had a range below required by the specification. Once it was ready, the Westinghouse AN/APQ-35 radar was installed in the third prototype. This system in fact consisted of three radars:

- a search radar, AN/APS-21 in 'X' band. It was used by the radar operator to locate targets within a range of 20 nautical miles (32 km);
- the AN/APG-26 fire control radar. This acquired the target within a range of two nautical miles (3.2 km) as the target approached and if it was necessary to open fire. This radar was used by the pilot on reception of the first details provided by the radar operator who, meanwhile, continued to look out for other potential targets using the AN/APS-21.
- the AN/APS-28 rear warning radar, added on the F3D-2. This provided warning of a target approaching from the rear in terms of distance, direction and height. This radar had a range of 4 nautical miles (6.4 km.).

At the beginning of the 1950s, this system was the best available in terms of detection capability. The first series production aircraft took to the air on 13 February 1950. It was accepted by the Navy and joined the inventory as from August 1950. On 5 December 1950, VC-3 based at Moffet Field in California became the first Naval unit to receive the F3D-1. Douglas test pilot La Verne Brown assisted the unit's naval officers with orientation flights on the following day. Following VC-3, Skyknights were delivered to VMF(N)-52 at El Toro, this being a US Marine Corps night fighter unit, and to the NATC.

*The F3D-2Q Skyknights of VMCJ-2 lined up. The first is "CY/16" BuNo127050. (Richard Dann Collection via J. Fernandez)*

The aircraft was considered to be underpowered, but the J46 engines intended to replace the J34 were never fitted due to recurrent development problems. As a result, an improved version of the J34 (J34-WE-36/36A) giving a thrust of 3,400 lb (1,540 kg) was fitted. This gave an increase of maximum speed to 600 mph (960 km/h) and extended the range of action to 1,200 miles (1,920 km).

An F3D-2 equipped with these engines first flew in 1951 and 237 of this type were manufactured. Only 28 F3D-1 (the initial order) were produced and, as these were considered underpowered, they were used for conversion of pilots onto the F3D-2. The most noticeable other differences between the F3D-2 and the F3D-1 were the air intakes, deflectors to aid tighter turning manoeuvres, a tail radar, a General Electric G-3 auto-pilot, an armoured windscreen and an improved air conditioning system.

*The F3D-2T2s "198" and "195" of VF-121 at NAS Miramar in 1960. Both machines wear the paint scheme adopted in 1959 by the US Navy for jet trainers. (Richard Dann Collection via J. Fernandez)*

# XF3D-1

Prototype aircraft, three were built.

*The first prototype XF3D-1 (BuNo 121457). (Richard Dann Collection via J. Fernandez)*

*Two photos of XF3D-1 numbered 457 during tests at NAS Patuxent River (Maryland), June 1949.*
*(Both Richard Dann Collection via J. Fernandez)*

XF3D-1 prototype during tests.
(All Richard Dann Collection via J. Fernandez)

*The XF3D-1 (BuNo 121457) in flight. (Richard Dann Collection via J. Fernandez)*

*The XF3D-1 "458" with Sparrow I missiles. This photo was retouched to improve clarity before the image was released. (US Navy)*

# F3D-1 (F-10A)

Two-seat all weather day or night-fighter variant, powered by two Westinghouse J34-WE-32 turbojet engines. A total of 28 F3D-1s were manufactured under a contract signed in 1948. From 1962 the designation was changed into F-10A.

*This F3D-1 (BuNo 123743) was used for carrier trials between October 1949 and February 1950. (US Navy)*

*Above:* The F3D-1 (BuNo 123744) used by NATC from 1950 to 1956. Later this aircraft was transferred to China Lake for more testing.
*Below:* Early F3D-1 (possibly BuNo 123749) which was used for tests. Note engine intake covers and canopy hatch in open position. (Both Richard Dann Collection via J. Fernandez)

The F3D-1 (BuNo 123743) with code TT-13 under the windscreen. This aircraft was used for carrier trials between October 1949 and February 1950. External fuel tanks attached. (US Navy)

F3D-1 (BuNo 123763) of VC-3 in flight over San Francisco on 9 March 1951. It was the first squadron to receive production versions of the Skyknight.

F3D-1 (possibly BuNo 123743) lands aboard a carrier during tests at the beginning of the 1950s.

F3D-1 during ground maintenance. (Richard Dann Collection via J. Fernandez)

*Above: Officers of the British Royal Navy before the F3D-1 Skyknight used for carrier trials. Note the White Ensign on the mast.*
*Below: Early F3D-1 Skyknight with folded wings. Note the NATC markings. (Both Richard Dann Collection via J. Fernandez)*

*The first production F3D-1 (BuNo 123741).*

*F3D-1 (BuNo 123743) on the tarmac at NAS Patuxent River, 1952. This third
production aircraft took part in early carrier trials and later was modified to
a missile-armed F3D-1M and was used for tests at China Lake and Point Mugu.*

*F3D-1 (BuNo 123751) at NAS Patuxent River. This aircraft was converted to an
F3D-1M. Note the engine intake lips painted red. (All Richard Dann Collection via
J. Fernandez)*

*F3D-1 (BuNo 123763) used at NAS Glynco for training during 1962 and 1963. Earlier this aircraft served with VC-3. (All Richard Dann Collection via J. Fernandez)*

*F3D-1 (BuNo 123757) loaded with a Sidewinder EX-0 missile under the right wing and a "target" five-inch HVAR rocket under the left wing, 18 May 1953. Note the lack of tailhook and orange wing panels.*

*The XF3D-1 (BuNo 121458), reconfigured as the F3D-1M prototype, fires a Sparrow missile.*

# F3D-1M (MF-10A)

A certain number of F3D-1s (probably 12 machines) were modified to carry AIM-7 Sparrow guided missiles. To this end, four pylons were fitted under the wings.

*This F3D-1M (BuNo 123758) was used for tests of Sparrow 2 missiles in January 1958 at the Naval Missile Center, Point Mung (California). (Both Richard Dann Collection via J. Fernandez)*

F3D-1M (BuNo 123747) at Chine Lake in September 1957. Note the Radioplane XKDR-1 target on the underwing pylon. Note that on the photo below the aircraft is in the same configuration, but without the name Point Mugu on the tail and without the number on the nose. (Richard Dann Collection via J. Fernandez)

Skyknight with Sparrow 1 missiles tested by VX-4, Naval Missile Center, Point Mung (California). (Richard Dann Collection via J. Fernandez)

# F3D-2 (F-10B)

The specifications for the F3D-2 were set out in a letter of intent published in October 1949. The object of this was to improve the performance of the Skyknight through fitting more powerful engines. When it made its first flight, the F3D-2 had two J34-WE-36 (or J34-WE-36A) giving a thrust of 1,540 kg. This version was equipped with a General Electric G3 auto-pilot, a Westinghouse AN/APQ-36 interception radar, a fire-control radar, a new air-conditioning system and a strengthened armoured windscreen. A total of 237 F3D-2 were manufactured. The last one left the factory on 23 March 1952.

*F3D-2 (BuNo 127059) at Douglas El Segundo in 1952 (or 1953). Note the description "Douglas F3D Skyknight" on the nose. (US Navy)*

*F3D-2 (BuNo 124598) was one of three Skyknights delivered to the Raytheon Corporation for testing radar systems in the late 1970s. Note the different marking. On the top photo aircraft is with ARMY marking and on the lower with NAVY marking. (Richard Dann Collection via J. Fernandez)*

*F3D-2 of VMF(N)-513 lined up. (Richard Dann Collection via J. Fernandez)*

*F3D-2 "LT/13" of VMF(N)-531 in flight. This unit was based at MCAS Cherry Point. (All Richard Dann Collection via J. Fernandez)*

*F3D-2 Skyknight (BuNo 127072) ATG/402 of VF-14 with 150-gallon tanks under the wings, ready to be launched. This squadron served aboard USS Intrepid and USS Forrestal.*

*F3D-2 "ATG/403" of VF-14 on the deck of USS Intrepid (CVA-11) during carrier qualifications in November 1954.*

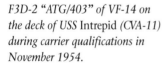

*Douglas F3D-2, No.127038, of VF-11 (US Navy), 1954. Aircraft in overall Sea Blue Scheme.*

*Douglas F3D-2, No.124650, of VMF(N)-531 (US Marine Corps) in September 1951. Aircraft in overall Sea Blue Scheme.*

*Douglas F3D-2 No.127072, of VF-14 (US Navy), 1955. Aircraft in overall Sea Blue Scheme.*

*An F3D-2 on the deck of USS* Midway *(CV-41) during suitability tests conducted between July and December 1951. (Richard Dann Collection via J. Fernandez)*

*F3D-2 (BuNo 124596) is preparing to launch. After trials with NATC this aircraft served with VX-5 and finally was converted to an EF-10B and was used by VMCJ-3. (Richard Dann Collection via J. Fernandez)*

The NATC F3D-2 with number 742 takes off during carrier trials.

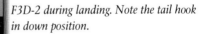

F3D-2 during landing. Note the tail hook in down position.

A landing signal officer guides an F3D-2 of VMF(N)-531.
(All Richard Dann Collection via J. Fernandez)

**Above:** *Skyknight (BuNo 127062) "T/402" of VF-14 lands on the deck of USS* Forrestal *with Deputy Secretary of Defense Reuben B. Robertson Jr. as passenger. VF-14 used the F3D for carrier qualifications only.*

**Below:** *F3D-2 (BuNo 125874) "T/405" on USS* Forrestal *with Assistant Navy Secretary J.H. Smith Jr. as passenger. (Both Richard Dann Collection via J. Fernandez)*

*Above: Formation of Skyknights of VX-4 in flight over NAS Point Mugu in the mid 1950s. (US Navy)*

*Left: Skyknight (BuNo 127038) which was delivered from the Douglas factory to the US Navy as the first F3D-2M and later may have operated with VF-11. (US Navy)*

*One of the Raytheon Skyknights (BuNo 124598) in flight, late 1970s. (Richard Dann Collection via J. Fernandez)*

*F3D-2 of VMF(AW)-542, late 1950s. This squadron continued to train night fighter crews with Skyknights until 1959.*

*F3D-2 of VMF(N)-531, late 1950s. In that period the tail code was changed from LT to EC.*

*F-10B (BuNo125807) at China Lake, May 1961. Note the orange-white markings applied to training aircraft. (All Richard Dann Collection via J. Fernandez)*

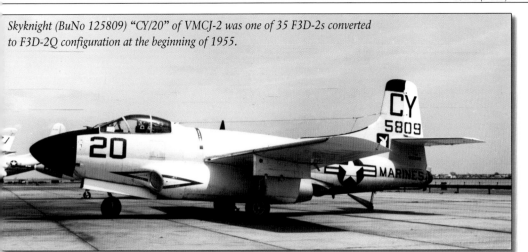

*Skyknight (BuNo 125809) "CY/20" of VMCJ-2 was one of 35 F3D-2s converted to F3D-2Q configuration at the beginning of 1955.*

**Left:** *The F3D-2 (BuNo 124642) which served with the Naval Parachute Facility at El Centro (California), July 1960.*

**Below:** *F3D-2 "T/414" of VF-14 after a mid-air collision on 18 November 1955 returned safely to NAS Cecil Field. (All Richard Dann Collection via J. Fernandez)*

*F3D-2 (BuNo 127072) overflies USS Intrepid in November 1954. Aircraft with external fuel tanks. Note extended arrester hook and flaps in landing position.*

*F3D-2 "NA/74" on the deck of USS Roosevelt, early 1950s. Later this aircraft was converted to an F3D-2Q/EF-10B and was operated by VMCJ-1 and VMCJ-3. (Both Richard Dann Collection via J. Fernandez)*

*F3D-2 "T/412" of VF-14 in the air in 1953. (Richard Dann Collection via J. Fernandez)*

*Douglas F3D-2, No.124642, of VC-4 (US Navy) embarked on board USS Midway in 1952–1953. Aircraft in overall Sea Blue Scheme.*

# F3D-2B

In 1952 the Skyknight was modified for special armament tests (missiles and nuclear weapons). Modifications for the nuclear-carrying F3D included the removal of the two left cannons and the tail warning radar. Equipment for special bombing was added. The wing pylons were reinforced to allow the aircraft to carry either one MK-7 or one MK-12 nuclear bomb. Skyknight BuNo 127044 was the only prototype for this variant of the F3D-2. In 1953 the aircraft was delivered to VX-5.

*F3D-2B (BuNo 127044) of VX-5, 18 October 1953, NAS Oakland. (Both Richard Dann Collection via J. Fernandez)*

# F3D-2M (MF-10B)

Sixteen F3D-2s were modified to carry AIM-7 Sparrow air-to-air missiles. Four hard points were fitted below the wings and the nose cone was enlarged. This was the first US Navy aircraft to be fitted with air-to-air missiles guided by the crew. The four cannons were removed.

*Above:* The first F3D-2M (BuNo 127038) with four wing pylons and extended nose, housing the APS-36 radar.

F3D-2M (BuNo 125847) of VMF(N)-542 with Sparrow missiles, 1957. (Both Richard Dann Collection via J. Fernandez)

*F3D-2M with tactical number 882 at NAMC Point Mugu, April 1961. Note the ACEL description on the tail and red tail markings. Earlier this aircraft served with VMF(N)-531. (Richard Dann Collection via J. Fernandez)*

*Excellent photo of F3D-2M shows off all the Skyknight's belly details.*

*The YF3D-2M (BuNo 127028), former Naval Missile Test Center aircraft, rests in storage at Davis Monthan AFB (MASDC), early 1960s. (Both Richard Dann Collection via J. Fernandez)*

*F3D-2M (BuNo125872)
"WH/15" of VMF(AW)-542.
late 1950s. (Richard Dann
Collection via J. Fernandez)*

*Douglas F3D-2M, No.125872, of VMF(AW)-542 (US Marine
Corps). Aircraft with modified nose.*

# F3D-2Q (EF-10B)

Following tests carried out on an F3D-2 in 1955, some 35 aircraft were modified on behalf of the Marines for use on electronic counter measures (ECM) activities and electronic intelligence gathering (ELINT). Once their cannon and combat radar had been removed, the F3D-2s had a huge internal volume available which could accomodate all kinds of electronic warfare equipment. They were used in Vietnam.

*Above:* Formation of F3D-2Qs from VMCJ-3 in flight, 12 May 1958. Three of these aircraft (BuNos 125806, 125850 and 127060) served later in Vietnam with VMCJ-1. 125806 was lost in action.

*Left:* The F3D-2 (BuNo 125786) which was in late 1955 reconfigured as the second prototype F3D-2Q. (Richard Dann Collection via J. Fernandez)

*EF-10B (BuNo 125810) of VMCJ-1 in 1966 on the deck of a transport carrier. (Richard Dann Collection via J. Fernandez)*

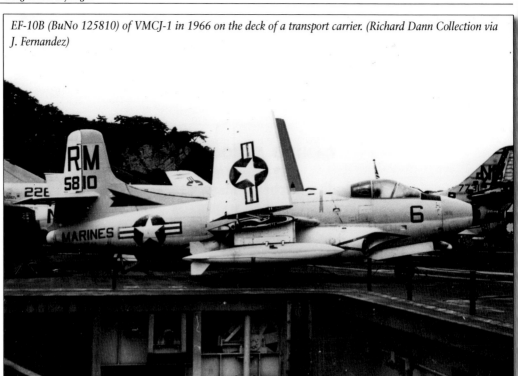

*EF-10B (BuNo 127041) "RM/7" of VMCJ-1. (Richard Dann Collection via J. Fernandez)*

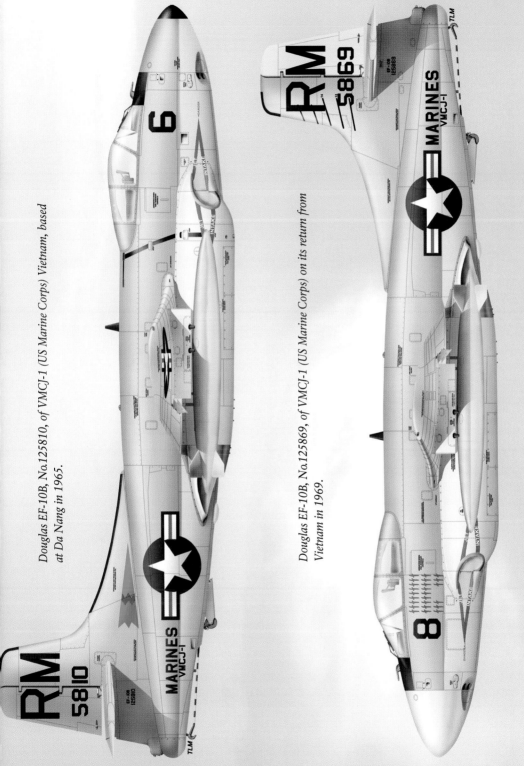

*Douglas EF-10B, No.125810, of VMCJ-1 (US Marine Corps) Vietnam, based at Da Nang in 1965.*

*Douglas EF-10B, No.125869, of VMCJ-1 (US Marine Corps) on its return from Vietnam in 1969.*

Formation of F3D-2Q Skyknights of VMCJ-3 in flight over Japan, on 12 May 1958.

EF-10B (BuNo 127060) "TN/10" of VMCJ-3. (Both Richard Dann Collection via J. Fernandez)

*Above: The first prototype F3D-2Q (BuNo 124620) "RM/2" at MCAS El Toro, California.*

*Skyknights of VMCJ-2 – the first airplane is EF-10B BuNo 124618 "CY/18". This aircraft was equipped with external ECM pods and chaff dispensers.*

*EF-10B (BuNo 125846) "TN/5" of VMCJ-3. (All Richard Dann Collection via J. Fernandez)*

*Above:* F3D-2Q (BuNo 127047) "CY/16" of VMCJ-2 at NAS Patuxent River in December 1965. This squadron was used in ELINT missions over Cuba, monitoring radar and radio signals from 1960 to 1962.

*Below:* EF-10B (BuNo 125846) "TN/5" of VMCJ-3 at MCSA El Toro during the mid-1960s. (Richard Dann Collection via J. Fernandez)

# F3D-2T & F3D-2T2 (TF-10B)

The F3D-2T was a night fighter training version, for which ten aircraft were modified (BuNos 124595, 124605, 124607, 124622, 124627, 124635, 124638, 124629, 124658 and 127022). Another 55 Skyknights were designated F3D-2T2 and were used to train radar operators for the McDonnell Douglas F-4 Phantom, and also as an electronic warfare trainer. The F3D-2T was equipped with Westinghouse AP-50 radar, while the F3D-2T2 used the AN/APG-51B radar (later also APG-51C).

*In May 1958 the FAWTUPAC was changed into VF(AW)-3. Photos show the F3D-2T2 (BuNo 125824)*
*"PA/143" with new designation on the aft of the fuselage. All photos were taken at NAS North Island in 1961.*

*The F3D-2T2 (BuNo 125824) at NAS North Island, 1961.*

*The FAWTUPAC F3D-2T2 "PA/21" in flight, late 1950s.*

*Skyknight "PA/14" prepares to depart from NAS North Island in 1958. This airplane was used for carrier trials at the beginning of the 1950s. (Both pages Richard Dann Collection via J. Fernandez)*

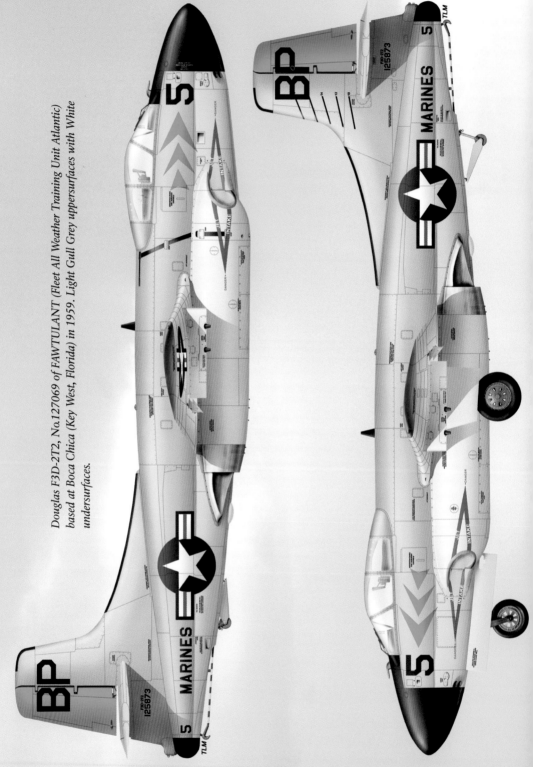

*Douglas F3D-2T2, No.127069 of FAWTULANT (Fleet All Weather Training Unit Atlantic) based at Boca Chica (Key West, Florida) in 1959. Light Gull Grey uppersurfaces with White undersurfaces.*

*Douglas F3D-2T2, No.125819, of VF-101 (US Navy), in April 1961. Light Gull Grey uppersurfaces with White undersurfaces.*

*Douglas F3D-2T2, No.125873, of VMFT(N)-20, 1959. Aircraft in overall Sea Blue Scheme.*

**Above:** *F3D-2T2 of VF-101 "AD/180" in August 1958. VF-101 was based at NAS Oceana, Virginia. The aircraft is overall glossy sea blue with FAWTULANT yellow markings.*

**Left:** *F3D-2T2 (BuNo 127083).*

**Below:** *F2D-2T2 (BuNo 125870) "PA/17". September 1955. (All Richard Dann Collection via J. Fernandez)*

Douglas F3D-2T2, No.127048, of VF-101 (US Navy), a training unit for radar operators, 1959. Aircraft in overall Sea Blue Scheme.

Douglas F3D-2T, No.124658 of US Marine Corps service unit MAG-24 in 1959. Light Gull Grey uppersurfaces with White undersurfaces.

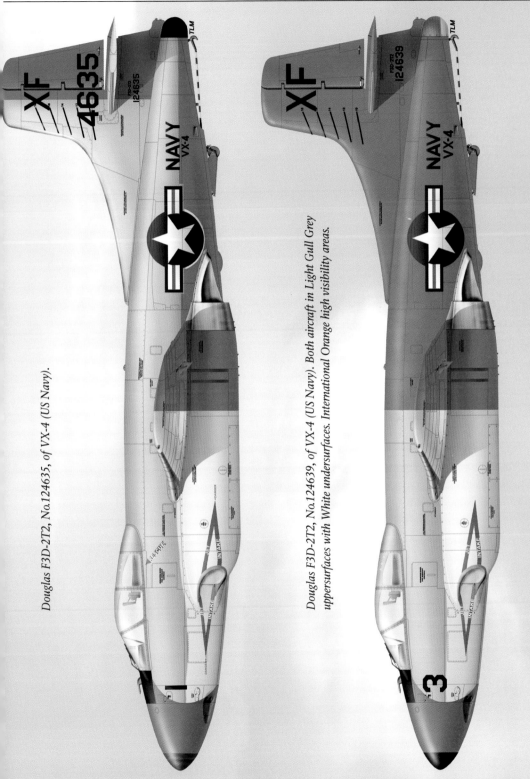

*Douglas F3D-2T2, No.124635, of VX-4 (US Navy).*

*Douglas F3D-2T2, No.124639, of VX-4 (US Navy). Both aircraft in Light Gull Grey uppersurfaces with White undersurfaces. International Orange high visibility areas.*

The F3D-2T2 (BuNo 125807) operated by Raytheon Corporation. This aircraft was used in tests between 1969 and 1981, when a wheels-up landing ended its career and it became a spare parts source for other Skyknights used by Raytheon. Note the different markings – ARMY and NAVY. F2D-2T2 (BuNo 125870) "PA/17". September 1955. (All Richard Dann Collection via J. Fernandez)

Another F2D-2T2 (BuNo 124630) operated by Raytheon Corporation in the 1970s and mid-1980s. This plane also had both ARMY and NAVY markings.

The F3D-2T2 "NJ/198" at NAS Miramar, June 1960. This unit used Skyknights to train F3H pilots and F4H Phantom II pilots and Radar Intercept Officers (RIO). (All Richard Dann Collection via J. Fernandez)

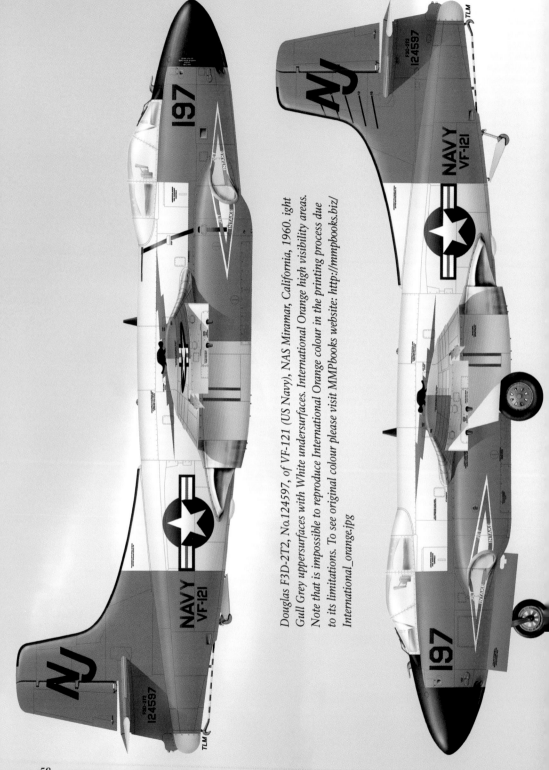

Douglas F3D-2T2, No.124597, of VF-121 (US Navy), NAS Miramar, California, 1960. ight Gull Grey uppersurfaces with White undersurfaces. International Orange high visibility areas. Note that is impossible to reproduce International Orange colour in the printing process due to its limitations. To see original colour please visit MMPbooks website: http://mmpbooks.biz/ International_orange.jpg

*F3D-2T2 "NJ/194".*

*F3D-2T2 (BuNo 124597) of VF-121 at NAS Miramar in about 1961. Note the lightning bolt and turtle emblem on the fuselage. (All Richard Dann Collection via J. Fernandez)*

*Above:* F3D-2T2 (Bu 124639) "XF/3" of VX-4, at NAS North Island in September 1959.
*Left:* TF-10B (BuNo 124630) with A-4 Skyhawk nose at China Lake, 16 March 1967. Four Skyknights had modified noses to test new radar systems. (Both Richard Dann Collection via J. Fernandez)
*Below:* TF-10B (BuNo 127074) at China Lake, 16 March 1967. The unusual nose housed the AN/APQ-89 terrain-following radar. (René Francillon)

# F3D-3

The F3D-3 was the designation assigned to a planned swept-winged version of the Skyknight. This version was to have been powered by the J46 turbojet. Because of the cancellation of the J46 project, calculated performance of the F3D-3 with the substitute J34 was deemed insufficient to warrant production. The order for 287 production F3D-3s was cancelled in February of 1952 before any could be built.

# KOREAN WAR

One of the first missions given to Skyknights was to escort B-29 formations. The latter were moving over to night operations after having suffered considerable losses at the hands of MiG-15s during daytime raids.

The advantage of darkness did not last for long since the Soviets supplied ground-based interception radars and their crews, which allowed close control of the MiG pilots who began to intercept B-29s at night. At first, the USAF tried using F-94 Starfires but their limited radar capabilities prevented them from providing an effective barrier between the bombers and MiG-15s operating from Manchuria.

*F3D-2 "WF/2" numbered 12 7/8 of VMF(N)-513 at Pohang (K-3) airfield, 1954. The number was closest to the so-called "unlucky 13". (Richard Dann Collection via J. Fernandez)*

*A pair of Skyknights of VMF(N)-513 take off from an unidentified airfield in Korea, 1952.*

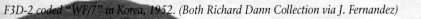

*F3D-2 coded "WF/7" in Korea, 1952. (Both Richard Dann Collection via J. Fernandez)*

The Soviet GCI ground radar detection system proved able to guide the interceptors through gaps in the bomber stream, thus allowing the MiGs to calmly make a firing pass through the bomber formations and then returning northwards over the frontier before the F-94s could react.

Given the feeble success of the system and mounting B-29 losses, the Marines were asked to act as escorts. The enemy GCI was unable to distinguish between the B-29s and the F3Ds and, thanks to this advantage, the latter were able to score several night time victories without loss to themselves. Even though its aerodynamic qualities left much to be desired and it was inelegant compared with the MiG-15, the Skyknight was heavily armed and very manouverable but, above all, it had workable radar, while the MiG pilots, who had to depend on ground control, were practically blind.

*F3D-2 Skyknight "WF/2" on a Korean airfield.*

*Skyknight on a runway somewhere in South Korea. (Both Richard Dann Collection via J. Fernandez)*

*The nose cone of a Skyknight of VMF(N)-513 open for ground crew to check the electronic systems. (Richard Dann Collection via J. Fernandez)*

On the night of 2-3 November 1952, a Skyknight flown by Major William Stratton, with Master Sergeant Hans Hoglind as radar operator, announced that they had shot down what they had identified by its trail as a Yak-15, even though this type never served in North Korea and never saw combat. The victory was classified as certain since the Skyknight flew through a cloud of debris and closely avoided damage to itself. This was the first victory at night of a jet over another jet, though it turned out to be doubtful since, according to Soviet archives, the MiG pilot succeeded in extinguishing the fire on board and returning to his base, the aircraft itself flying again after five days of repairs. Five days later, at 1:30 in the morning of 7 November another Skyknight flown by Captain O.R. Davis, with Warrant Officer D.F. "Ding" Fessler as radar operator, shot down an MiG-15. The MiG pilot, Lt. Kovalyov, was able to eject.

While the F3D appeared somewhat clumsy looking, it was not so in practice and a MiG which decided to join a turning combat with it could soon find itself on the wrong end. The F3D's combination of an armaments system and a powerful battery of four 20 mm cannon could prove fatal to enemy fighters. The advantage of the arms system was illustrated on 10 December 1952, when an F3D piloted by Lt. Joseph Corvi, with Master Sergeant Dan George as radar operator, spotted an adversary on the radar and gained one of the first successes in BVR mode. The enemy in question turned out to be one of the small Po-2 biplanes used for harassing United Nations forces at night, a task which it accomplished to perfection. The Po-2 was nevertheless a difficult target since it flew low and slow and its wooden airframe did not show up well on the radar. But as no friendly air-

*Above:* F3D-2 "WF/20" of VMF(N)-513 at Pohang airfield.

*Left:* Radar operator SSgt. Eugene "Mule" Holmberg of VMF(N)-513 at Pohang (K-3) airfield, 1953.

*Below:* F3D-2s of VMF(N)-513 at Kunsan airbase. The jet engine air intakes are protected to prevent entry of foreign objects. (All Richard Dann Collection via J. Fernandez)

*F3D-2 "WF/22" of VMF(N)-513 in flight. After the Korean War this unit was moved to Japan and based at NAS Atsugi. (Richard Dann Collection via J. Fernandez)*

craft was officially indicated in the sector, Corvi did not hesitate and one can only imagine the result of firing a battery of 20mm cannon against an aircraft made largely of wood and canvas.

In total, Marine Skyknights claimed six victories, mostly MiG-15s, and no B-29 flying under their protection was brought down by enemy fighters. Two Skyknights were lost in combat for unknown reasons.

But there were occasions on which extreme measures were required to avoid being shot down, though the F3D's strength proved up to the task. For example, Capt. George Kross recounted an experience while flying a mission in January 1953 – this was the closest an F3D came to being brought down by an enemy fighter.

With the Skyknight's tail radar out of service, the MiG-15, guided to the rear of the night fighter, was able to approach closely and score a succession of rapid hits on Kross's F3D. If he had been warned in time, he would have been able to take evasive action and reduce the risk of being hit. The very high speeds induced by a vertical dive led to problems with the controls.

Later examination of the rear of Kross's aircraft led to some very interesting conclusions. During the debriefing, Kross stated that the MiG followed him down during his high speed dive and fired a few more rounds, leading the experts to conclude that the enemy pilot would not have been able to follow the F3D's evasive manoeuvres unless his aircraft was fitted with an on-board radar. In fact, in its issue of 9 February 1953, Aviation

*F3D-2 "WF/3" landing at Kimpo Air Base in 1953. (Richard Dann Collection via J. Fernandez)*

*Douglas F3D-2, No.124620, of VMF(N)-513 (US Marine Corps) based at Pyong Taek, Korea, 1953. Aircraft flat black overall with dull red markings.*

*The F3D-2 "WF/9" of VMF(N)-513.*

*F3D-2 "WH/23" of VMF(N)-542. (Both Richard Dann Collection via J. Fernandez))*

Douglas F3D-2, No.127030, of VMF(N)-513 (US Marine Corps) Korea, based at Pohang airfield in September 1953. Both aircraft flat black overall with dull red markings.

Douglas F3D-2 of VMF(N)-513 (US Marine Corps). Crew: Lt.Col. R.F.Conley (2 victories over MiG-15s) and M/Sgt. J.N.Scott, Korea, March 1953.

Week published an article confirming that night fighter MiG-15s were operating with radar, thus constituting a permanent menace for United Nations aircraft operating night missions.

Concerning the damage inflicted on Kross's aircraft, both he and his radar operator (R/O) were lucky to live to tell the tale. Inspection showed many cannon strikes on the aircraft's tail surfaces, with one passing directly between the two engines and piercing 19 successive fuselage frames before finally ending up jammed above the escape hatch located between the pilot and his R/O. A direct hit like that on one of the two engines would have proven fatal to the F3D and its crew.

Shipboard use of the F3D by the Navy was limited to almost the end of the war. This was due to the aircraft carriers' flight decks being too short and to their need to operate multi-role aircraft such as the F9F Panther. VC-4 (Det.44N) operated four F3D-2s from USS *Lake Champlain* (CVA-39), which arrived in Korean waters during the last few months of the war. Within the combat zone, this detachment made several sorties from the carrier and some from land while it was attached to VMF(N)-513.

*Right: Lt-Col. Robert F. Conley explains how he shot down a MiG-15 on 31 January 1951. This was to be the tenth and final victory scored by VMF(N)-513 during the Korean War.*
*Below: F3D-2s of VMF(N)-513 in flight over Korea, late 1953 or early 1954. F3D-2 "WH/23" of VMF(N)-542. (Both Richard Dann Collection via J. Fernandez)*

Victories obtained by VMF(N)513 Skyknights during the Korean War

| 3 November 1952 | Maj. W. Stratton Jr. M. Sgt. H. G. Hoglind | Yak-15 * |
|---|---|---|
| 8 November 1952 | Capt. O. R. Davis WO D. F. Fessler | MiG-15 |
| 10 December 1952 | Lt. J. A. Corvi M. Sgt. D. R. George | Po-2 |
| 12 January 1953 | Maj. J. P. Dunn M. Sgt. L. J. Fortin | MiG-15 |
| 28 January 1953 | Capt. James Weaver M. Sgt. Becker | MiG-15 |
| 31 January 1953 | Lt.Col. Robert Conley M. Sgt. J. N. Scott | MiG-15 |
| 2 July 1953 | Lt.(jg) R. S. Bick ATC Linton Smith | MiG-15 |

\* It is now known that the aircraft was in fact a MiG-15 and that it was only damaged.

**Above:** *A pair of Skyknights of VMF(N)-513 in flight over Korea in late 1953 or early 1954. Note the heavy weathering on F3D-2 number 8.*

**Left:** *Major Elswin P. "Jack" Dunn and MSgt. Larry Fortin of VMF(N)-513 describing the combat with a MiG-15 on 12 January 1953. (Both Richard Dann Collection via J. Fernandez)*

*Skyknight of VMF(N)-513 "WF/18" (BuNo 127027) with blue colour scheme and white code and numbering. (Both Richard Dann Collection via J. Fernandez)*

*F3D-2 of VMF(N)-513 prepared for a night sortie over Korea.*

# ELECTRONIC WARFARE

It has been noted that 55 F3D-2s were converted into electronic warfare aircraft whose duties were to pinpoint and neutralise enemy radar transmissions. Now designated F3D-2Q, they equipped three Marine Reconnaissance Composite Squadrons – VMCJ-1, VMCJ-2 and VMCJ-3 – with which they served alongside F-9 Cougar and F-8 Crusader photographic reconnaissance aircraft. A typical mission was to fly in a straight line along a predetermined route over the suspected radar station. During the flight, the electromagnetic signal detector and signal analyser showed up the size, type and range of the radar station. On return from mission, the information collected was analysed and the position of the radar station was approximately determined. Following this, photo-reconnaissance aircraft were sent into the zone to identify the precise location of the station.

Once its position had been accurately determined, the station could be neutralised either by active or passive means. In the first case, fighter bombers were sent to destroy it and in the second, Skyknights were called in again. The F3D-2Q had two ways of jamming the radar station, either by sending out electromagnetic signals or by launching metallic chaff capable of saturating radar signals.

During the Formosa crisis of 1957/1958, these aircraft were the first to detect anti-aircraft defence fire control systems of the Peoples' Republic of China. At the end of the 1950s Lt. Colonel Reid of VJCM-3 was instrumental in carving out a peacetime electronic reconnaissance role for the nine F3D-2Qs deployed to Japan. He was able to convince the Commander-in-Chief Pacific to allow the aircraft to join the Peacetime Aerial Reconnaissance Program (PARPRO) and the squadron began to fly missions over North Korea, Russia and China under the nickname "Sharkfin". These kind of missions were usually flown by a pair of F3D-2Qs staging out of bases at Misawa in Northern Japan, Osan (Korea) and Tainan (Taiwan). These sensitive missions were tightly controlled and required detailed reporting. The Electronic Intelligence (ELINT) collected tape recordings of intercepted radar signals that were forwarded to the Pacific Command (PACOM) centre at Fuchu in Japan, along with hand

*EF-10B "TN/9" of VMCJ-3 in early 1960s. (Richard Dann Collection via J. Fernandez)*

*EB-10B "CY/16" of VMCJ-2. Note the Playboy Bunny emblem on the tail.*

drawn plots of radar locations and signal characteristic data logged by the electronic counter measure operator (ECMO). The "Sharkfin" missions not only furnished information on the employment of radars used during the Cold War by America's adversaries, but also provided an excellent training environment for VMCJ aircrews.

Later on, during the Cuban missile crisis, the EF-10Bs (as Skyknights were designated from 1962), were the first to detect the presence of Soviet radars on the island. During operations against Cuba VMCJ-2 became the first Marine unit to be awarded a Navy Unit Commendation in peace time for its electronic and photo reconnaissance missions tracking the build-up of Soviet supplied military capabilities in communist Cuba from September 1960 through to the end of the Cuban Missile Crisis, in December 1962. The squadron began to fly ELINT missions around Cuba in 1960 (no doubt the success of the "Sharkfin" missions was an important

*F3D-2Q (BuNo 124645) in flight with an RF-8A of VMCJ-3.*
*(Both Richard Dann Collection via J. Fernandez)*

factor for starting such flights). These unofficial missions staged out of Key West, Guantanamo Bay and other Caribbean airfields were later sanctioned and controlled by the Peacetime Aerial Reconnaissance Program by US Navy Commander in Chief Atlantic Fleet (CINCLANT). The initial intercepts were mainly of air traffic control radars, but as the Soviets steadily increased the flow of Cuban air defence system in 1961, F3D-2Q aircrews of VMCJ-2 began to intercept military radars.

*Formation of Skyknights of VMCJ-3 over Mt. Fuji, Japan, 12 May 1958. (Richard Dann Collection via J. Fernandez)*

# VIETNAM WAR

In April 1965, VMCJ-1 embarked its EF-10Bs stationed at the US Marine Corps base at Iwakuni for Vietnam, where they joined the Marine Aircraft Group. Skyknights of VCMJ-1 began their wartime missions from 17 April 1965. They formed part of the means set up to counteract the deployment of ground-to-air missiles in Vietnam.

The Skyknights also flew escort missions for bombing raids over North Vietnam. After being in intensive service for several months, including attack missions, they were then relegated to support duties on behalf of Air Force and Naval aircraft flying over high risk zones such as SA-2 missile launching sites. In July 1965, six EF-10B Skyknights of VMCJ-1 supported the first strike against a surface-to-air missile site in history.

They played a full operational role in *"Rolling Thunder"* missions over North Vietnam. By the end of 1965, Skyknights had carried out 791 support missions over Laos and North Vietnam. In November 1966, the first Grumman EA-6A Intruder was introduced at Danang and flew combat missions as far north as Hanoi and Haiphong and eventually phased out the EF-10Bs.

By the end of 1970, all Skyknights had been withdrawn from service with operational units. Several aircraft nevertheless continued to serve as flying test beds with Raytheon up until the 1980s.

*EF-10B "RM/5" of VMCJ-1 in flight. (Both Richard Dann Collection via J. Fernandez)*

*Skyknight (BuNo 125809) "RM/8" landing at Da Nang, February/ March 1967.*

*EF-10B (BuNo 125849) with 30 EW mission marks, Da Nang, February/March 1967.*

*F3D-2 (BuNo 125786) of VMCJ-3 before being reconfigured as the second prototype F3D-2Q, late 1955.*

*EF-10B (BuNo 124632) "RM/3" at Da Nang in February/March 1967. Note the two EW mission marks under the canopy and the small 9 on the rudder. (Both Richard Dann Collection via J. Fernandez)*

# F3D Skyknight operators

VC-3 (tail code NP)

Created in May 1948, this squadron was based at Moffet Field (California) as from the following September. The unit's purpose was to train pilots and maintenance personnel. Being resposible for crew transformation onto new equipment, it was the first Navy unit to receive the F3D-1.

*The airship hangar floor at NAS Moffett Field, 13 October 1952. Note the different types of aircraft: F3D Skyknight, F2H-2 Banshee and F4U Corsair – all from VC-3.*

*F3D-1 Skyknights of VC-3 lined-up at NAS Moffet Field, California, June 1951. (Both Richard Dann Collection via J. Fernandez)*

### VX-4 (XF)

Air Development Squadron Four was formed on the East Coast in 1950. Its initial mission was to develop airborne radar alert systems. Its next mission was to evaluate guidance systems for air launched missiles and to allow the fleet to optimise available equipment.

The first project given to VX4 was the development of the Sparrow I missile. The F3D Skyknight was the first aircraft type designated for this missile. Tests continued wth the Sparrow II and other missiles. As a result, the Skyknight remained in service with the Naval Missile Center at Point Mugu (California) until the 1960s.

In the beginning, an XF3D-1 was converted for missile launching. Following this, two F3D-1s were modified as F3D-1Ms to continue testing which proved successful and led to the conversion of 16 F3D-2s into F3D-2Ms. The latter were transferred to VMF(N)542 which became the first operational squadron to be equipped with guided missiles.

### VX-5 (XE)

This experimental unit had the task of evaluating and perfecting air-ground missiles. An F3D-2 was among the various aircraft equipping this squadron.

### VC-4 (NA/C)

This was the Navy's only Skyknight squadron to spend time at sea on aircraft carriers. It embarked on the Coral Sea and other carriers in 1952 and on the Midway in 1952/53. Although based at Atlantic City in New Jersey, it spent time at sea in both the Atlantic and Pacific, its mission being to protect the fleet from air attack at night and in all weathers.

### VF-14 (T/ATG)

This unit converted onto the F3D-2 in January 1954. At the beginning of 1956, these were replaced by the F3H-2N Demon. VF-14 did not have time to deploy the F3D but was able to carrier qualify in the type aboard the USS Intrepid in November 1954.

*F3D-2 (BuNo 127038) "ATG/404", 9 November 1954. Note the unit emblem on the fuselage.*
*(Richard Dann Collection via J. Fernandez)*

*Skyknight "ATG/404" just after take off from the deck of USS* Intrepid *(CVA-11). 13 October 1954.*

*Skyknight of VF-14 in the water. Piasecki HUP-2 helicopter is going to rescue the crew. (Both Richard Dann Collection via J. Fernandez)*

*Formation of three F3D-2s (T/101, T/102 and T/104) of VF-14 in flight, September 1954. (Both Richard Dann Collection via J. Fernandez)*

## VF-11 (T)

This squadron was equipped with the Skyknight between 1953 and 1956 and like VF-14 would not deploy aboard a carrier.

## VC-33 (SS)

Composite squadron operating out of NAS Atlantic City, New Jersey. This squadron was equipped with Skyknights at the begining of the 1950s.

*Skyknight "SS/2" of VC-33, 24 November 1952. (NARA)*

## FAWTUPAC /VF(AW)-3 (PA)

This unit was originally activated as NACTUPAC in August 1944. In 1946 the squadron started a series of name changes cumulating in August 1948 as FAWTUPAC and in May 1958 VF(AW)-3. This unit, based on the Pacific coast (NAS Moffett Field, NAS North Island) was intended for training personnel in all-weather operations. It was equipped exclusively with the Skyknight between 1953 and 1958. Even though the F3Ds were officially replaced by the F4D Skyray in 1958, they continued to fly with the squadron until March 1963.

*FAWTUPAC crew climb into F3D-2T2 "PA/11" during a staged alert at NAS North Island (near San Diego, California) in 1958.*

*Pilot and radio operator (RO) rush to a Skyknight in a staged alert at NAS North Island, 1958. (Both Richard Dann Collection via J. Fernandez)*

*FAWTULALT Skyknight "LP/6" at Boca Chica Field in the 1950s. (Richard Dann Collection via J. Fernandez)*

## FAWTULANT (LP/HG)

The Fleet All Weather Training Unit Atlantic was based at Boca Chica Field, Key West in Florida. This unit had the same mission as the above, but intended for personnel on the Atlantic coast. Skyknights operated with this unit during the 1950s.

## VF-121 (NJ)

In 1958 VF-121 became the permanent air replacement unit on the West Coast. Its task was to prepare pilots and maintenance crews for shipboard service. VF-121 was equipped with F11F-1, F3H-2N, F2H-4 and the F3D-2T2. Among other duties, the Skyknights were charged with training radar interception operators (RIO) destined for service on the F3H Demon. The F3D-2T2s (TF10B) continued to serve until 1965, by which time a sufficient number of F4Ds had become available.

*Skyknights of VF-121 at NAS Miramar, early 1960s. (Richard Dann Collection via J. Fernandez)*

### VF-101 (AD)

This unit was the Atlantic Coast equivalent of VF-121. It had ten F3D-2T2s for RIO radar training. As a training squadron this unit was based at NAS Oceana, Virginia.

### NAS Glynco VT-86 (4B)

This unit was occupied with training RIO operators destined for F4s serving with VF-121 and VF101. Skyknights were used for this purpose up to 1965.

*F3D-1 (BuNo 123761) "WH/2" of VMF(N)-542. (Both Richard Dann Collection via J. Fernandez).*

*F3D-2 (BuNo 127049) "WH/10" of VMF(N)-542, 30 July 1955.*

## VMF(N)-542 (WH)

This was the first Marine Corps unit to evaluate the XF3D-1 in 1948. It received its Skyknights in 1951. These were F3D-1s to begin with, followed by F3D-2s. Once it had been reequipped, the unit was sent to Korea where it arrived on 18 June 1952. A few days later, 14 of the 15 aircraft were repainted in matt black. Soon afterwards, the Skyknights were handed over to VMF(N)513. On its return to the United States, VMF(N)542 was re-equipped with the F3D-2M, thus becoming the first missile armed fighter squadron. The Skyknights were replaced by the F4D Skyray in 1959.

## VMF(N)-513 (WF)

This unit was set up as a night fighter squadron in August 1947. It was engaged in Korea at the beginning of Autumn 1950, being equipped at the time with the F4U-5N Corsair and the F7F-3N Tigercat. In June 1952 it received the Skyknights of VMF(N)542, but the unit only became fully operational on 1 November 1952. The mission of the 12 Skyknights was to ensure the escort of US Air Force B-29s carrying out night time raids. The North Korean MiG-15s used a tactic intended to eliminate the danger posed by the Skyknights. This involved flying through the bomber formation and trying to get chased by the American night fighters. Once a Skyknight was out of the formation, two other MiG-15s jumped on its tail. This strategy did not work as the MiGs were detected by the Skyknight's tail alert radar and it was able to get out of the way before the MiGs got within cannon fire range.

*F3D-2 "WF/24" of VMF(N)-513 crewed by 2nd Lt. Donald Harvey and S.Sgt. Donald Lambert, South Korea, September 1954. (Richard Dann Collection via J. Fernandez)*

Duties were not only limited to interception by night. On 27 March 1953, the Skyknights took part in an attack on Chinese artillery positions using conventional bombs. This kind of operation was repeated on 10 April.

At the end of May 1953, VMF(N)513 had 24 Skyknights on charge and the last Tigercats were withdrawn. During its time in Korea, VMF(N)513 lost two aircraft and their crews for reasons which remain mysterious.

### VMF(N)-531 (LT/EC)

This was the first US Marine Corps night fighter squadron. It received its first F3D-1s in January 1952 while based at Cherry Point and was assigned the mission of training pilots and radar operators for duty with VMF(N)-513 in Korea. These served alongside Corsair and Tigercat night fighters.

*Skyknight "LT/3" of the VMF(N)-531. This unit received its first F3D in January 1952. (Richard Dann Collection via J. Fernandez)*

### VMF(N)-20 (LP/BP) and 10

According to many sources both these units operated Skyknights, but little is known of their career. With no doubt VMF(N)-20 was equipped with F3D-2 in late 1950s when based at Cherry Point. But it is hard to find photographic proof of the existence of Skyknights in VMF(N)-10.

### VMCJ-1 (RM)

In total 55 F3D-2 aircraft were converted to F3D-2Q Skynights. Such aircraft were able to locate and neutral-ize hostile radar transmissions. In this role the F3D-2Q (EF-10B) was operated by three Marine Reconnaisance Composite Squadrons – VMCJ-1, VMCJ-2 and VMCJ-3.

VMCJ-1 took Skyknights to war on 17 April 1965, when the squadron deployed six EF-10Bs jets to Danang from Iwakuni (Japan). The Skynights' mission was to jam enemy radar while escorting air strikes into North Vietnam. The aircraft were also attacking ground forces on their return flights. Hoewever these attacks were very costly and soon were stopped, as the Skynights did not have ejection seats or sufficient power to exit the target area at high speed.

VMCJ-1 was very active over Vietnam during May and June of 1965. Because of lack of spare parts, from July the activity of VMCJ-1 was much lower. The Skyknight missions were limited to support Air Force and Navy operations in only high threat areas. The primary targets were the positions of SA-2 missiles. A major contribution was made by the squadron's machines during "Rolling Thunder" missions over North Vietnam. During these missions, VMCJ-1 provided support in the ECM and electronic intelligence (ELINT) roles under the code name "Fogbound". In 1969, the Skyknights of VMCJ-1 were replaced by the A-6A Intruder.

### VMCJ-2 (CY)

VMCJ-2 was commissioned at MCAS Cherry Point (NC) on 12 December, 1955 and has a claim to being the first VMCJ squadron. It was the result of the merger of VMJ-2 and VMC-2 bringing together the photo reconnais-

*EF-10B (BuNo 124632), "CY/16" of VMCJ-2 at MCAS Cherry Point 11 October 1968. (Both Richard Dann Collection via J. Fernandez)*

sance and electronic warfare squadrons that had been operating as part of the 2nd Marine Aircraft Wing since the Korean War. Initially the squadron began operating the F9F-6P Cougar photo reconnaissance and AD-5N ECM aircraft. The AD-5Ns were replaced by the F3D-2Q Skyknight for EW operations beginning in 1957.

VMCJ-2 was the first Marine unit to be awarded a Navy Unit Commendation in peace time for its electronic and photo reconnaissance missions tracking the buildup of Soviet supplied military capabilities in communist Cuba from September 1960 through the end of the Cuban Missile Crisis in December 1962. In late November 1965, VMCJ-2 received the first EA-6A Intruder.

### VMCJ-3 (TN)

VMCJ-3 was commissioned on 12 December, 1955 at MCAS El Toro (CA). It marked the merger of VMC-3 and VMJ-3 which consolidated the 3rd Marine Aircraft Wing's electronic warfare and photo reconnaissance capabilities into a single squadron.

VMCJ-3 inherited the two prototype F3D-2 Skyknights that had been undergoing conversion to electronic warfare variant by VMC-3 avionics personnel to provide the Marine Corps its first tactical jet electronic warfare (EW) platform. In February 1956 both prototypes (124620 and 125786) were officially designated as F3D-2Q

*EF-10B (BuNo 127034) "TN/1" of VMCJ-3. (Richard Dann Collection via J. Fernandez)*

After the successful testing of the ECM suite a recommendation was made to the Director of Aviation, HQMC to modify 36 F3D-2s based on the prototype configuration with 12 to be assigned to each of the VMCJ squadrons.

In August, 1957, Lt. Colonel Robert Reid took over as commander. He began to prepare the squadron to deploy to MCAS Iwakuni, Japan in August of 1958 for a 15 month tour. This was the first operational deployment of a VMCJ squadron and the last for VMCJ-3.

Lt. Colonel Reid was instrumental in carving out a peacetime electronic reconnaissance role for the nine F3D-2Qs deployed to Japan. He was able to convince the Commander-in-Chief Pacific to allow the aircraft to join the Peacetime Aerial Reconnaissance Program (PARPRO) and the squadron began to fly missions along the periphery of North Korea, Russia, and China under the nickname "Sharkfin".

In November 1959 the VMCJ-3 returned to MCAS El Toro where it remained until decommissioned in August 1975. From 1960 until 1965 this unit served as the main training squadron. In June, 1970, the last EF-10B on the Marine Corps inventory (125618) was flown to Quantico where it remains till today.

**Other USMC units (utility squadrons):**
Hedron FMF PAC – tail code W2
Hedron-12 – tail code WA
MAMS-24 – tail code AW
SOS-3/H&HS-3 – tail code LU
H&HS – tail code AZ
H&HS-27 – tail code B2
H&HS-24 /MAG-24 – tail code EW
MARS-37 – tail code QF

*Douglas F3D-1, VMF-542 in flight.*

*FAWTUPAC F3D-2T2 at North Island, late 1950s.*
*(Both Richard Dann Collection via J. Fernandez)*

# Skyknight survivors

**F3D-2 Skyknight, BuNo *124598*,**
    is on display at the National Museum of Naval Aviation in NAS Pensacola, Florida.

**F3D-2Q Skyknight, BuNo *124618*,**
    is on display at the USMC Museum, in Quantico, Virginia.

**F3D-2Q Skyknight, BuNo *124620*,**
    is under restoration for display at the Quonset Air Museum in Quonset Point, Rhode Island.

**F3D-2 Skyknight, BuNo *124629*,**
    is on display at the Pima Air & Space Museum in Tucson, Arizona.

**F3D-2Q Skyknight, BuNo *124630*,**
    is on display at the Flying Leatherneck Historical Foundation in Miramar, California.

**F3D-2 Skyknight, BuNo *125807*,**
    is on display at the Combat Air Museum in Topeka, Kansas.

**F3D-2Q (later EF-10B) Skyknight, BuNo *125850*,**
    is under restoration for display at the Air Force Flight Test Center Museum at Edwards AFB, California. When operational, this aircraft served until 1970 as part of VMCJ-3 (Marine Composite Reconnaissance Squadron 3) based at Marine Corps Air Station El Toro, carrying tail code "TN."

**F3D-2 Skyknight, BuNo *125870*,**
    (marked as BuNo *127039*), is mounted on a display pylon at the Vietnam War memorial in Del Valle Park in Lakewood, California. It is painted in the 1960s-era grey and white color scheme of Marine aircraft. The aircraft bears the tail code "7L," which was the 1960s-era tail code designated for Marine Air Reserve Training Detachment and Naval Air Reserve aircraft based at Naval Air Station Los Alamitos.

**F3D-2T Skyknight, BuNo *127074*,**
    was on display at the USS *Intrepid* Museum in New York City, New York until April 2012. It will be moved to the Empire State Aerosciences Museum near Schenectady, NY. (Operated by Raytheon in Massachusetts as an electronics test plane until it was donated to the museum in 1987. It is painted in the colors of Marine night fighter squadron VMFN-513 as flown during the Korean War.)

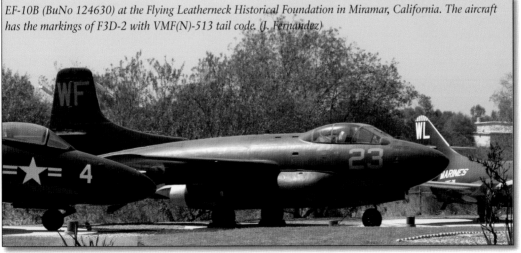

*EF-10B (BuNo 124630) at the Flying Leatherneck Historical Foundation in Miramar, California. The aircraft has the markings of F3D-2 with VMF(N)-513 tail code. (J. Fernandez)*

*F3D-2 ATG/409 in the markings of VF-14. USS Intrepid Museum. (J. Fernandez)*

# Douglas F3D Skyknight Technical Description

by Paul E Eden

The F3D Skyknight was a two-seat, twin-engined, all-metal, mid-winged all-weather naval fighter

**Wing:** Straight cantilever wing with 3° dihedral and folding for carrier stowage. Before wing folding could commence the spoilers had to be returned to their neutral position, manually prior to BuNo. 125791 and via a control in the cockpit from that aircraft onwards; a safety mechanism prevented wing folding with a spoiler extended, since the folded outer panel would foul an extended spoiler. Hydraulic wing folding and spreading was accomplished from the cockpit, requiring between 5 and 7 seconds for the wings to fully spread, after which a further cockpit action was required to secure the wing locking pins

**Fuselage:** All metal with plastic nose radome. Pilot and radar operator seated side-by-side in pressurised, air-conditioned cockpit with emergency escape chute to the lower fuselage. Regular cockpit access via a sliding panel in the upper canopy section; also used as a ditching hatch. One hydraulically actuated airbrake on either side of the fuselage, opening to full 45° deflection in 3 seconds and closing in 1 to 1.5 seconds. The airbrakes could be held at intermediate positions by releasing pressure on their control grip switch

**Cockpit enclosure:** Flak-resistant windscreen. A hatch in the cockpit roof was opened for access/egress, and as an emergency escape hatch in the event of ditching. Normal activation was manual, from inside the cockpit or externally, while emergency opening was via a 1,980psi (13651kPa) one-shot compressed air system. The lower escape chute hatch was jettisoned by air from the same system

**Tail:** The mid-set tailplane was mounted at an incidence of 2.5° nose-up

**Control surfaces:** Trim tabs were fitted to the rudder, port aileron and elevator, controlled from the pilot's left-hand console. The hydraulic wing flaps were controlled by a lever, also in the left console. BuNos 124595 to '664 had an emergency hydraulic flap extension system, while in aircraft after 125783, emergency extension was by air pressure. Aileron spoilers were installed on the wing upper surfaces, forward of the flaps and inboard

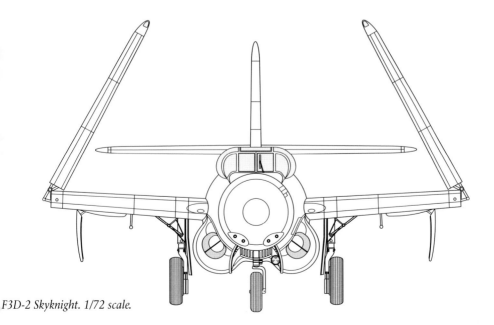

*F3D-2 Skyknight. 1/72 scale.*

of the wing fold lines. The spoilers opened when the control stick passed through 10° left or right of neutral, the port spoiler opening when the stick was left and vice versa. Power-boosted ailerons were fitted outboard of the wing fold on the folding wing panel

**Undercarriage:** Tricycle landing gear, with tail bumper, suitable for catapult-assisted take-off, with arrester hook under rear fuselage for arrested landings. Undercarriage activation was hydraulic, the tail bumper extending and retracting with the main gear. The undercarriage doors were also hydraulically activated. Emergency extension was by gravity. The hydraulically-boosted brakes were activated by toe pressure on the rudder pedals, twice the normal required pressure being sufficient to achieve braking in the event of hydraulic failure. The arrester hook was lowered by air pressure and retracted hydraulically

**Powerplant:** F3D-2: two Westinghouse J34-WE-36 or 36A turbojet engines, each rated at 3,400lb (15.12kN) static thrust located in nacelles either side of the lower centre fuselage and fed by two lateral air intakes

**Oil system:** An oil tank of 3.45US gal (13-litre) useable capacity was located outboard of each engine, low down in the forward section of the engine nacelle

**Fuel system:** Internal fuel was contained in three tanks mounted in the centre fuselage aft of the cockpit. Useable fuel quantities from front to rear were 650US gal/3,900lb (2461 litres/1769kg), 290US gal/1,740lb (1098 litres/789kg) and 410US gal/2,460lb (1552 litres/1116kg), respectively. One auxiliary tank with a useable capacity of 150US gal/900lb (568 litres/408kg) could be carried under each wing, for a maximum useable fuel capacity of 1,650US gal/9,900lb (6246 litres/4491kg)

**Hydraulic system:** The primary hydraulic system operated at 3,000psi (20684kPa), with a 400-2,500psi (2758-17237kPa) auxiliary system fitted for aileron power boost and spoiler operation. The auxiliary system could also be used for testing the main system on the ground and in emergency could deliver 3,000psi for flap operation

**Electrical system:** The 28-volt DC electrical system was supported by a 24-volt battery, accessible via the lower escape chute door, and engine-driven generators. Each engine drove one generator, delivering full voltage from around 48% engine speed (about 6,000rpm). External power for engine starting could be connected to

| F3D-2 Skyknight | |
|---|---|
| Length | 45 ft 5 in |
| Wing span | 50 ft |
| Folder wing span | 26 ft 10 in |
| Height | 16 ft 1 in |
| Wing area | 400 ft² |
| Wing loading | 61.5 lb/ft² |
| Empty weight | 14,989 lb |
| Loaded weight | 21,374 lb |
| Max takeoff weight | 26,731 lb |
| Engines | 2 x Westinghouse J34-WE-36 3,400 lbf (15 kN) each |
| Max speed(at sea level) | 580 mph |
| Range | 1,375 miles (with two 150 gal tanks) |
| Service ceiling | 36,700 ft |
| Rate of climb | 2,970 ft/min |
| Armament | 4 x 20 mm cannon with 800 rounds each4,000 pounds of bombs, rockets or fuel tanks |

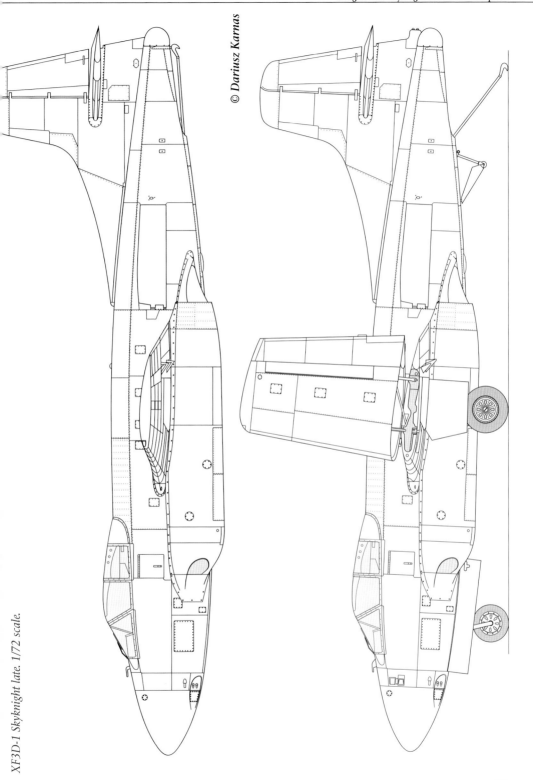

*© Dariusz Karnas*

*XF3D-1 Skyknight late. 1/72 scale.*

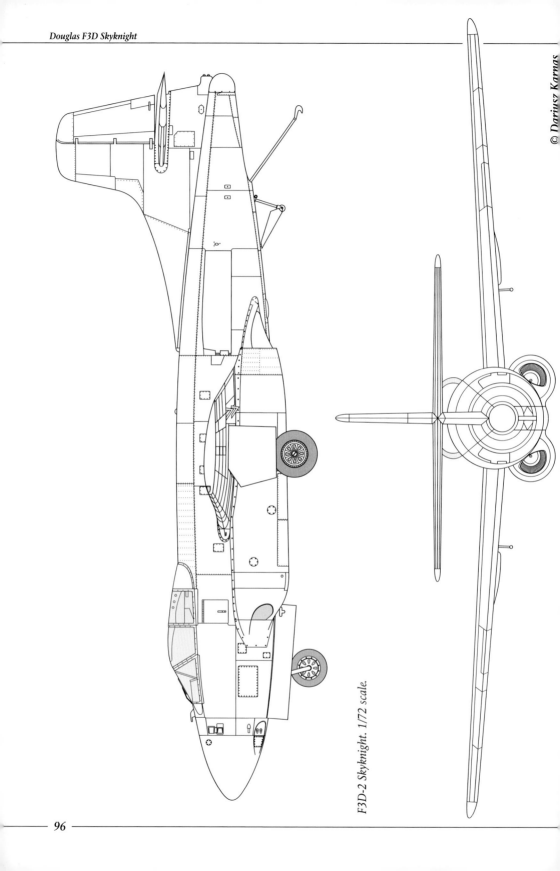

*F3D-2 Skyknight. 1/72 scale.*

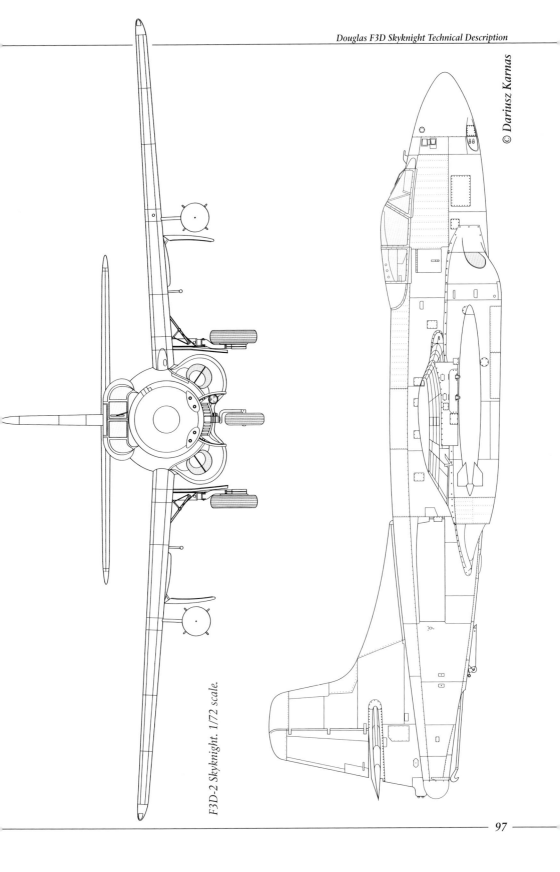

© *Dariusz Karnas*

*F3D-2 Skyknight. 1/72 scale.*

individual receptacles mounted in each main undercarriage bay on the rear spar. A second receptacle in the starboard bay, positioned alongside the engine-start receptacle, delivered external DC to the main aircraft electrical system

**Other systems:** Westinghouse AN/APQ-35 radar system comprising AN/APS-21 search radar, AN/APG-26 gun-aiming radar and AN/APG-28 tail-warning radar; BuNos 125822, '837, '847, '857, '867, '872, '877 and '882; 127023, '028, '043, '053 and '058 (F3D-2M) were equipped with Westinghouse AN/APQ-36 radar, compatible with the AAM-N-2 Sparrow I air-to-air missile (AAM). AN/APX-6 transponder or AN/APX-20 interrogator/responsor fitted for IFF

**Fixed armament:** four 20mm cannon in lower nose, aimed via a Mk 20 Mod 0 illuminated gunsight and AN/APG-26 radar. A gun camera was installed in the starboard wing inboard of the fold line

**Weapon carriers:** An Aero 61A 'supporting rack' (pylon) was installed beneath each wing for stores weighing up to 2,000lb (907kg). From BuNo. 125808, Mk 51 Mod 11 or Mod 12A stores racks could be used as alternatives. BuNos 125822, '837, '847, '857, '867, '872, '877 and '882; 127023, '028, '043, '053 and '058 had provision for launching AAM-N-2 Sparrow I AAMs

**Disposable stores:** Provision for one Mk 12, Mk 14 or Aero 1A auxiliary fuel tank containing 150US gal/900lb of useable fuel, or one 1,000lb general purpose (GP) bomb under each wing. Provision also made for 250, 500 and 2,000lb GP bombs, and 1,600lb armour-piercing bombs

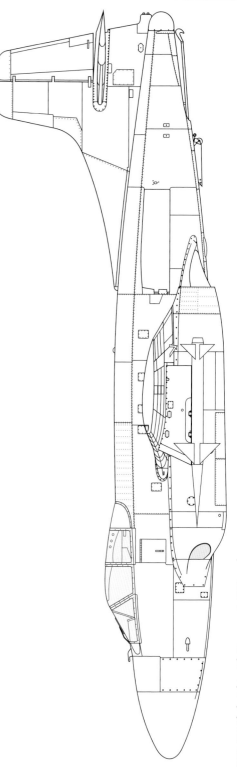

© Dariusz I          195

*F3D-2M Skyknight with Sparrow I. 1/72 scale.*

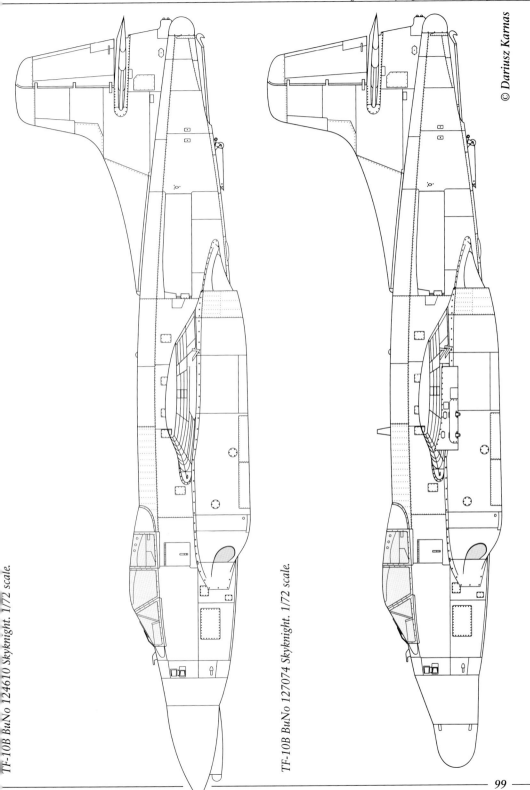

© *Dariusz Karnas*

*TF-10B BuNo 124610 Skyknight. 1/72 scale.*

*TF-10B BuNo 127074 Skyknight. 1/72 scale.*

# General View

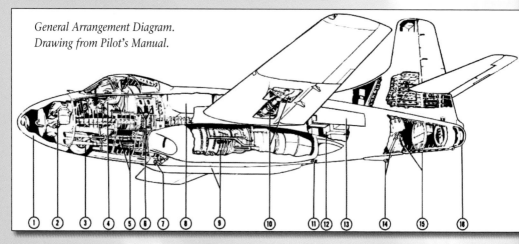

*General Arrangement Diagram.*
*Drawing from Pilot's Manual.*

1. Nose radome
2. Radar equipment compartment
3. Nose landing gear
4. Cockpit
5. 20 mm guns
6. Ammunition stowage
7. Catapult hook (both sides)
8. Fuel tank section
9. Jet engine installations
10. Main landing gear
11. Catapult hold back
12. Radio equipment compartment
13. Air brake
14. Tail bumper gear
15. Arrestor hook
16. Tail radome

*Early production F3D-1s of VC-3, which was the first Navy unit to recive this aircraft. Skyknights in formation flight over San Francisco in March 1951. (Richard Dann Collection via J. Fernandez)*

# Fuselage

*Two photos of the EF-10B (BuNo 124630) at the Flying Leatherneck Historical Foundation. Unique shape of the fuselage is visible. (J. Fernandez)*

*Above: Rear view of the EF-10B. Rear part of the fuselage is almost circular. AN/APS-28 transmitter/receiver was mounted in the rear fuselage. Arrester hook is removed. Big airbrakes panel is visible (with American Star). (J. Fernandez)*

*Below: Mooring system used on carriers. (Technical Manual drawing)*

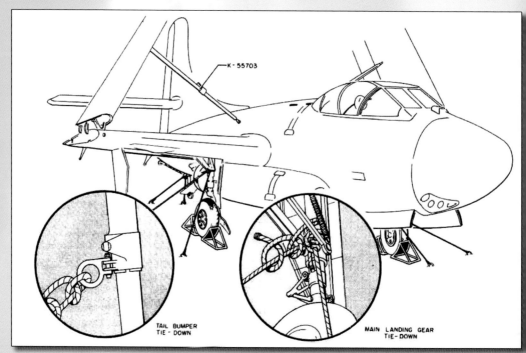

*Top:* Two photos of the engines inlets. Engine-fuselage intersection fairing is shown. Boundary layer bleed air duct is also visible in the right photo.

*Left:* Exhaust nozzle shroud details. Many aircraft had this nozzle unpainted due to high temperatures. Complicated fairing shape is also visible.

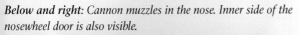

*Below and right:* Cannon muzzles in the nose. Inner side of the nosewheel door is also visible.

(All photos J. Fernandez)

*Front part of the fuselage, just in front of the cockpit. Pitot head is visible at the top.*

*Fuselage just behind the canopy. Footsteps are visible.*

*Front view of the Skyknight. Shape of the fuselage and engines are shown. Four cannon muzzles are also visible. (All photos J. Fernandez)*

**Top, left:** *Fuselage underside, navigation lamp is visible.*

**Top, right:** *Fuselage just below the cockpit. Air vent is visible.*

**Above, right:** *Details of the air vent, starboard side.*

**Above, left:** *Starboard side of the fuselage, below cockpit.*

**Below, left:** *Nose, lower part, starboard.*

*(All photos J. Fernandez)*

# Engine

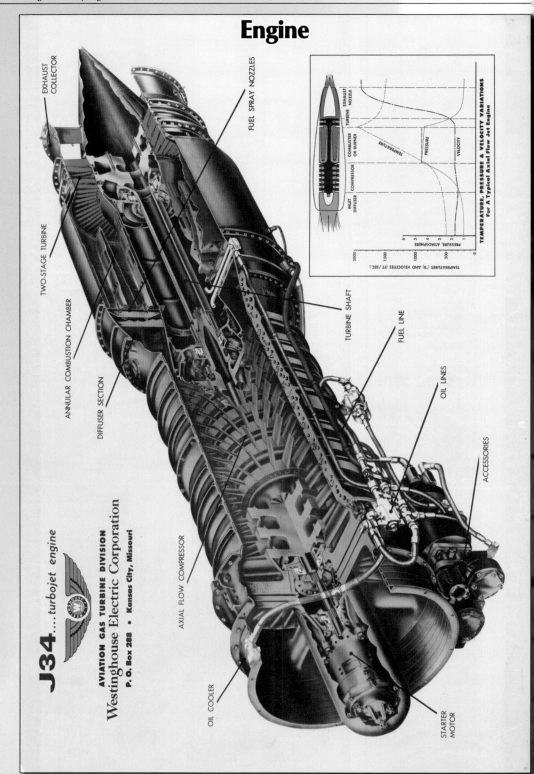

EXHAUST COLLECTOR

FUEL SPRAY NOZZLES

TWO-STAGE TURBINE

ANNULAR COMBUSTION CHAMBER

DIFFUSER SECTION

TURBINE SHAFT

FUEL LINE

OIL LINES

ACCESSORIES

AXIAL FLOW COMPRESSOR

OIL COOLER

STARTER MOTOR

**J34** ....*turbojet engine*

AVIATION GAS TURBINE DIVISION
**Westinghouse Electric Corporation**
**P. O. Box 288 • Kansas City, Missouri**

TEMPERATURE, PRESSURE & VELOCITY VARIATIONS
For A Typical Axial Flow Jet Engine

INLET DIFFUSER | COMPRESSOR | COMBUSTER OR BURNER | TURBINE | EXHAUST NOZZLE

TEMPERATURE

PRESSURE

VELOCITY

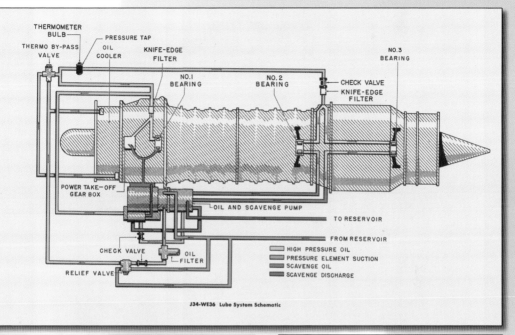

J34-WE36 Lube System Schematic

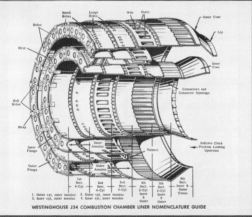

WESTINGHOUSE J34 COMBUSTION CHAMBER LINER NOMENCLATURE GUIDE

## J34-WE-46 COMPRESSOR HOUSING ASSEMBLY

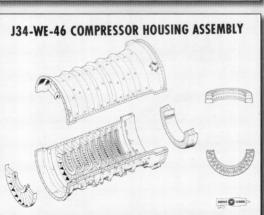

J34-WE-36 NO. 1 BRG. SUPPORT

*Both pages: Drawings from Engine Technical Manual.*

# Canopy

*Two photos showing profile of the canopy. Details of the nose are also visble, like air vents. Note complicated shape of the engine- fuselage intersection. (All photos J. Fernandez)*

*Starboard of the canopy. Note details of frame rivetting.*

*Flat plate windscreen panels. Pilot's windscreen wiper is also shown, just behind the pitot tube. Note differences in the inspection panels appearance.*

*Deatil shot showing the shape of the canopy side panels. Sliding cockpit entry hach was at the top of the canopy. (All photos J. Fernandez)*

*The NATC F3D-1 during trials, probably at NAS Patuxent River. Note the FT designation on the nose, April 1952. Sliding entry hood is in open position. (Richard Dann Collection via J. Fernandez)*

*Entrance to the Airplane.*

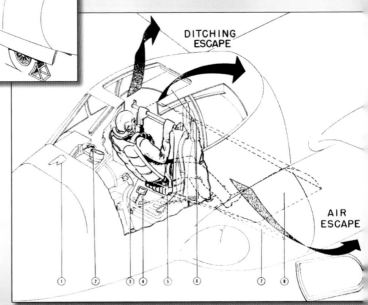

Emergency escape and exits. (Pilot's Handbook)

1. Pitot tube – barrier crash hook.
2. Upper escape hatch emergency release handle.
3. Back-type parachute.
4. Lower escape chute emergency release handle.
5. Pararaft kit.
6. Upper escape hatch.
7. Windscreen.
8. Lower escape chute.

Reloading the guns of an F3D-2T2. Details of the canopy frame are also visible, starboard side. Also note the stencils. (Richard Dann Collection via J. Fernandez

# Cockpit

*Miscellaneous Equipment Diagram.*
*(Pilot's Handbook)*

1. Airplane jack pad stowage.
1A. Radar Operator's foot transmit switch.
2. Radar Operator's foot rest.
3. Relief tube.
4. Ash tray.
5. Lap harness.
6. Radar Operator's seat.
7. First-aid kit.
8. Shoulder harness.
9. Shoulder harness inertia reel.
10. Radar Operator's assist handle.
11. Radar Operator's head rest.
12. Cockpit aft escape hand rail.
13. Pilot's head rest.
14. Pilot's seat.
14A Keying switch.
15. Map and oxygen mask stowage.
16. Personnel gear receptacle.
17. Radar Operator's chartboard.
18. Baggage stowage.

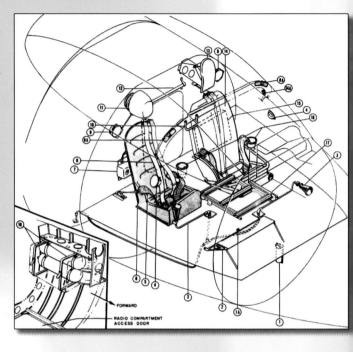

*Oxygen and Anti-G System Diagram.*
*(Pilot's Handbook)*

1. Pilot's oxygen regulator.
2. Radar Operator's anti-g air control.
3. Radar Operator's oxygen regulator.
4. Oxygen system filler valve.
5. Radar Operator's personnel gear receptacle.
6. Pilot's personnel gear receptacle.
7. Pilot's anti-g air control.
8. Oxygen cylinder.
9. Anti-g system air fiter.

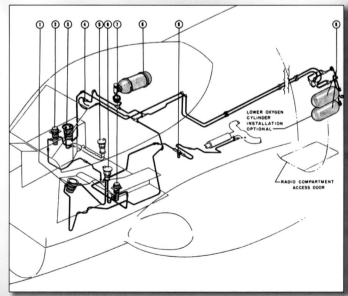

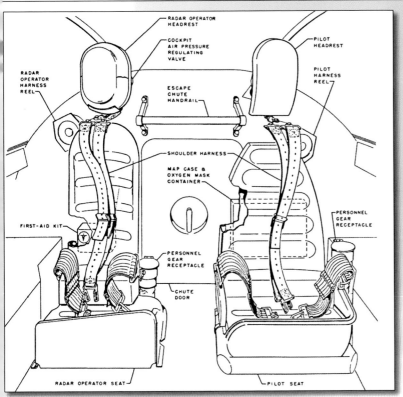

*Pilot's Handbook drawing showing cockpit equipment of F3D-1. Rear view.*

*Front view of the F3D-1 cockpit. (Pilot's Handbook)*

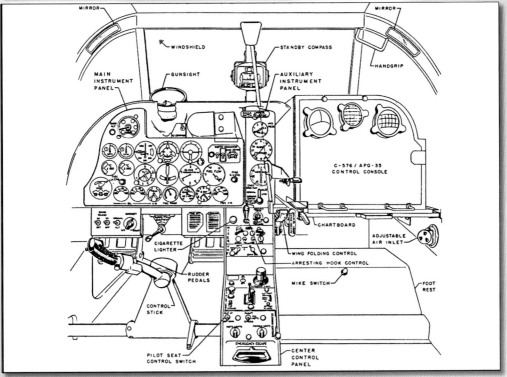

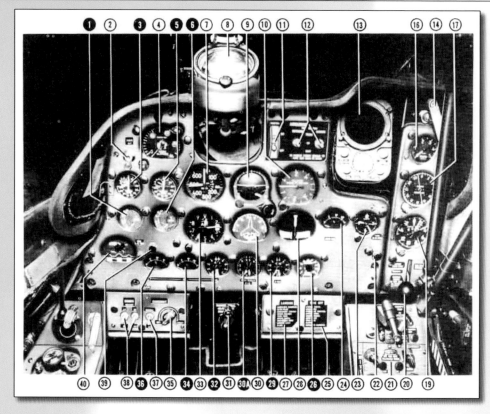

*Instrument Panel of F3D-1. (Pilot's handbook)*

1. Left-hand outlet temperature indicator.
2. Radio altimeter warning light.
3. Left-hand engine tachometer indicator.
4. Radio altimeter indicator.
5. Right-hand engine tachometer indicator.
6. Right-hand turbine outlet temperature indicator.
7. Airspeed indicator.
8. Gunsight.
9. Gyro horizon indicator – automatic pilot.
10. Rate of climb indicator.
11. Master armament switch.
12. Gun control switches.
13. AN APG-26 gun airning radar scope.
14. Upper escape hatch emergency release handle.
15. Deleted.
16. Hydraulic preassure gage.
17. AN ANR-6 radio compass indicator.
18. Deleted.
19. Accelerometer.
20. Auxiliary hydraulic system control.
21. Center console – see opposite page.

22. Right-hand engine fire warning light.
23. Clock.
24. Outside air temperature indicator.
25. Take-of check-off list.
26. Fuel quantity indicator.
27. Landing check-off list.
28. Turn and bank indicator – automatic pilot.
29. Mainfold fuel pressure indicator.
30. Master direction indicator – automatic pilot.
30A. Fuel boost pressure indicator.
31. Rudder pedal adjustment control.
32. Oil pressure indicator.
33. Altimeter.
34. Right-hand engine oil temperature indicator.
35. Gunsight light rheostat.
36. Left-hand engine oil temperature indicator.
37. Gunsight light selector switch.
38. Bomb selector switches.
39. Left-hand engine fire warning light.
40. Wheel and flap position indicator.

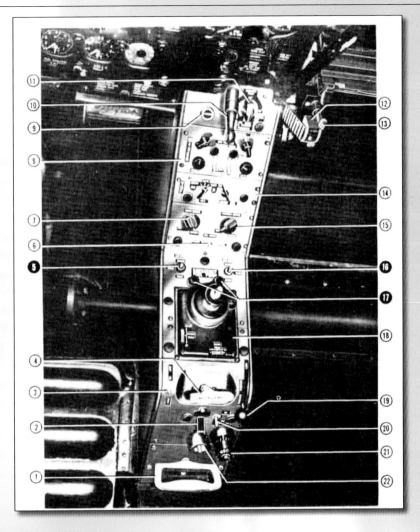

*Central console of F3D-1. (Pilot's handbook)*

1. Lower escape chute door emergency relese handle.
2. Apporoach light switch.
3. Pilot's seat adjustment switch.
4. Automatic pilot emergency release handle.
5. Left-hand engine emergency fuel pump switch.
6. Flight and instrument lights selector switch.
7. Instrument lights theostat.
8. Pilot's AN AIC-4 interphone control panel.
9. Cigarette lighter.
10. Arrestor hook control.
11. Air conditioning and cockpit pressurization control switch.
12. Wing folding control.
13. Aileron power boots emergency release.
14. Pilot's AN ARC-4 VHF radio control panel.
15. Left-hand and center console lights theostat.
16. Right-hand engine emergency fuel pump switch.
17. Fuel pump warning lights.
18. Automatic pilot controller.
19. Radar operator's shoulder harness control.
20. Extension light switch.
21. Extension light.
22. Automatic pilot clutch switch.

Radar Operator's Equipment of F3D-1.
Front View – Right Side

1. Chartboard light.
2. AN APQ-35 radar control panel.
3. Chartboard.
4. Fire warning test switches.
5. Radar operators's ventilating air outlet.
6. Right-hand console lights rheostat.
7. Generator warning light.
8. Left-hand generator volt-ammeter.
9. Right-hand generator volt-ammeter.
9A. Chartboard light.
10. Pitot heat switch.
11. Test jack panel.
12. Ash tray.
13. A-c power selector switch.
14. Right-hand circuit breaker panel.
15. Radar Operators's anti-g air control.
15A. Microphone headset extension cord.
15B. Oxygen regulator panel flood light.
16. Cockpit floodlight.
17. Radar Operator's oxygen regulator.
18. Exterior lights control panel.
19. AN APX-6 IFF radio control panel.
20. AN APX-2 IFF radio control panel.
21. Radar Operator's AN/ANC-4 interphone control panel.
22. AN ARC-28 VHF radio relay control panel.
23. Radar Operator's AN/ARC-1 VHF radio control panel.
24. Radar operator's relief tube.
25. AN ARR-2A VHF radio control panel.
26. Master radio switch.
27. Battery and generator switch.
28. Cabin altimeter.
29. Deleted.
30. Deleted.

**Opposite page:** Radar Operator's Equipment Right-Hand Console.

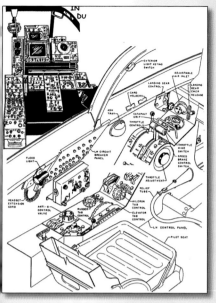

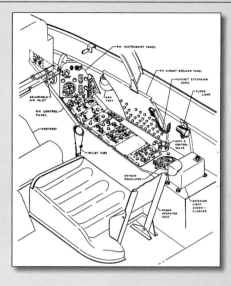

*Two drawings from Pilot's handbook showing cockpit details.*

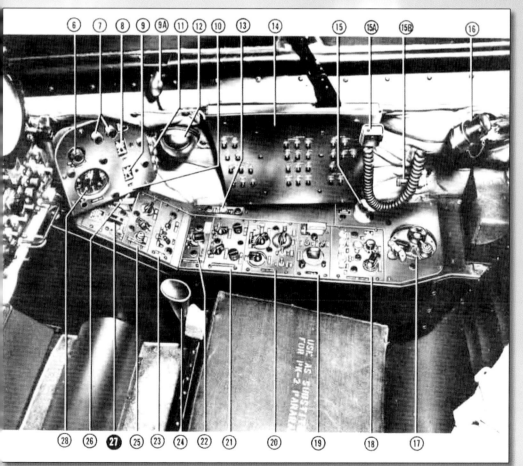

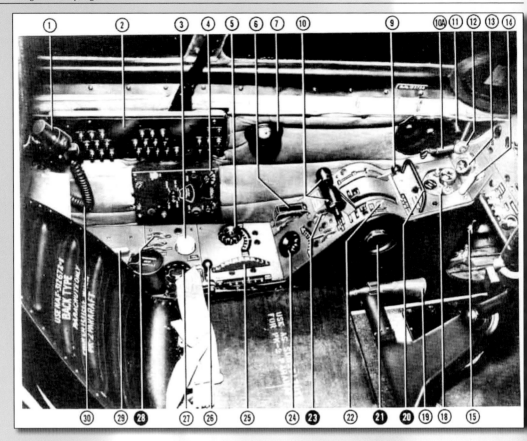

*Left-Hand Console. (Pilot's Handbook)*

1. Cockpit floodlight.
2. Left-hand circuit breaker panel.
3. Pilot's anti-g air control.
4. AN ARN-6 radiocompass control unit.
5. Rudder trim tab control.
6. Wing flap control.
7. Ash tray.
8. Deleted.
9. Gust lock control.
10. Throttle controls and radio – 1CS transmit switch.
10A. Oxygen regulator panel flood light.
11. Landing gear control safety lock.
12. Landing gear control.
13. Pilot's ventilating air outlet.
14. Landing gear emergency release handle.
15. Landing gear emergency control resset release.

16. Deleted.
17. Deleted.
18. Pilot's oxygen regulator.
19. Pilot's relief tube.
20. Throttle control static grip.
21. Throttle control friction adjustment.
22. Speed brake switch.
23. Master engine switch.
24. Aileron trim tab control.
25. Elevator trip tab control.
26. Pilot's shoulder harness control.
27. Altitude limit switch.
28. Fuel boots pump switches.
29. External store emergency release handle.
30. Microphone headset extension cord.

*ECM aircraft pilot's instrument*
*panel. (Pilot's Handbook)*

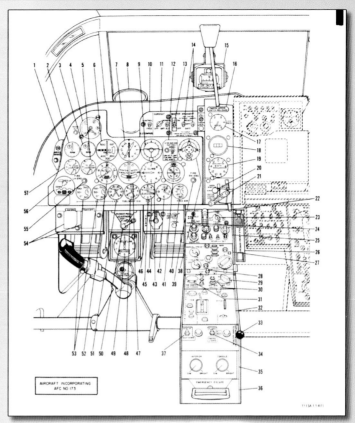

1. Speed Brake Position Indicator.
2. LH Engine Tachometer.
3. RH Engine Tachometer.
4. Radio Altimeter Indicator.
5. RH Turbine Outlet Temperature
   Indicator.
6. Air Speed Indicator.
7. Radio Magnetic Indicator.
8. Gun Sight.
9. Gyro Horizon Attitude Indicator.
10. G-2 Compass Control.
11. Gun Sight Control.
12. Gyro Horizon Fast Erect
    Warning Light and Switch.
13. Master Armament Switch.
14. Gun Control Switches.
15. Standby Compass.
16. Upper Hatch Emergency Release
    Handle.
17. Hydraulic Pressure Gage.
18. Distance Measuring Equipment.
19. Accelerometer.
20. Emergency Wing Flap Control.
21. Aileron Power Boost Release Handle.
22. Arresting Hook Control Handle.
23. Air Conditioning and Pressurization Control
    Switch.
24. Windshield Wiper Switch.
25. Radio ICS Control IAIC-4).
26. Wing Fold Control Handle.
27. UHF Radio Control (ARC-27).
28. UHF Selector Switch.
29. Inverter Selector Switch.
30. Power Failure Light.
31. Yaw Damper Relay Control.
32. Autopilot.
33. ECMO's Shoulder Harness Control Lever.
34. Pilot's Emergency Lights Switch.
35. Interior Lights Control.
36. Lower Escape Chute Door Emergency Release
    Handle.
37. Pilot's Seat Adjustment Switch.
38. Master Direction Indicator (G-2 Compass).

39. RH Engine Fire Warning Light.
40. Free Air Temperature Indicator.
41. Course Indicator.
42. Clock.
43. Vertical Speed Indicator.
44. Fuel Quantity Gage.
45. Fuel Quantity Gage Test Button.
46. TACAN Radio Control (ARN-21).
47. Turn and Slip Indicator.
48. Dual Fuel Boost Pressure Indicator.
49. Fuel Flow Indicator.
50. Rudder Pedal Adjustment Crank.
51. Dual Oil Pressure Gage.
52. Altimeter.
53. Oil Temperature Indicators.
54. Checkoff Lists.
55. LH Engine Fire Warning Light.
56. Wheels and Flaps Position Indicator.
57. LH Turbine Outlet Temperature Indicator.

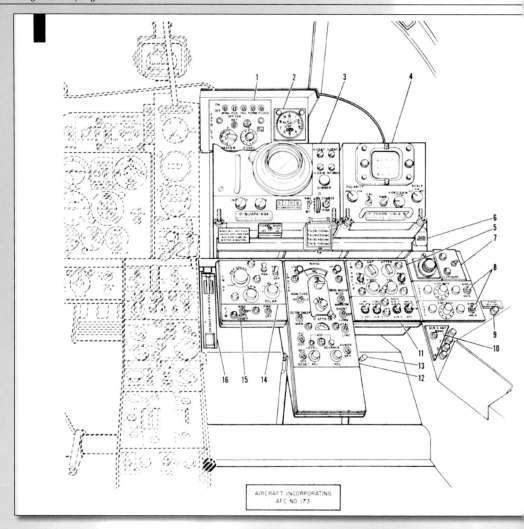

*ECM aircraft operator's instrument panel. (Pilot's Handbook)*

1. Exterior Lights Control.
2. Cabin Altimeter.
3. Azimuth-Panoramic Indicator (APA-H).
4. Pulse Anatyzer Indicatar (ALA-3).
5. ECM Receiver Control (ALR-31).
6. K-17 Camera Counter.
7. K-17 Camera Control.
8. Chaff Dispenser Controls (ALE-2).
9. Reel-End Warning Light (UNH-6).
10. Antenna Band Indicator (ALR-3).
11. ECM Mixer Box.
12. ECM Receiver Control(IAPR-9).

13. Foot Transmit Switch (AIC-4).
14. Direction Finder Control (APA-69).
15. Automatic Chaff Dispenser Control (ALQ-Z).
16. Wing Fold Control Handle.

# Wings

*Left*: XF3D-1, *in flight showing the wing platform Note the testing probe on the port wingtip. (Richard Dann Collection via J. Fernandez)*

*Below*: One of the first F3D-1s *in flight with air brakes extended. September 1950. Upper wing surface is visible. (US National Archives)*

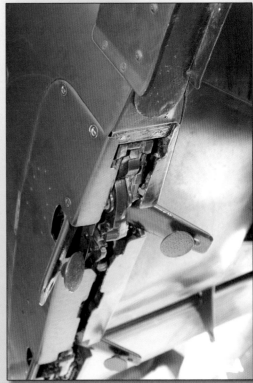

**This page:** *Three photos of the wing fold mechanism.*

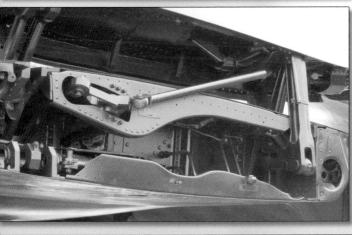

**Opposite page:** *Underwing pylon's details, bomb racks are visible. (All J. Fernandez)*

*Above:* Folding wing details.
*Below:* Landing flap in down position. Note flap airfoil. (Both. J. Fernandez)

*Air intake in thw starboard wing root.*

*Port wing tip fairing, rear view.*

*Starboard wing tip fairing, front view. Navigation light is visible. (All J. Fernandez)*

*Another two photos of the wing tips. Note the shape.*

**Bottom:** *Port wing from the rear. Flap in flying position. (All J. Fernandez)*

**Opposite page:** *Beautiful photo of the F3D-1 during overhaul. Details of the folding mechanism are visible. Also main undercarriage leg and wheel are shown. Aircraft with heavy weathering. (Richard Dann Collection via J. Fernandez)*

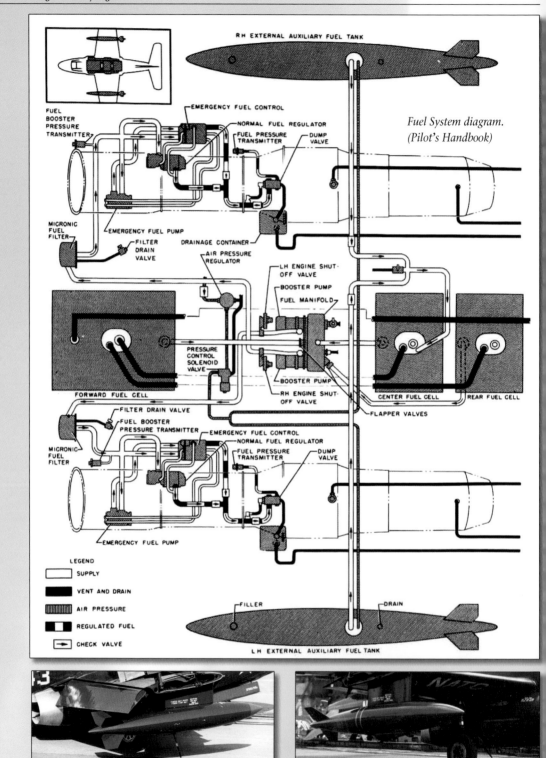

*Fuel System diagram.*
*(Pilot's Handbook)*

# Tail

**Top photos:** *Side views of the Skyknight tail. Tailwheel/bumper is visible.*

**Bottom.** *Elevator details. Elevator trim tabs actuators are visible. (All J. Fernandez)*

**Opposite page, bottom:** *Two photos of the external fuel tanks. (Richard Dann Collection via J. Fernandez)*

*Above: Starboard side of the vertical fin, below the elevator.*
*Right: Rear view of the tail.*
*Below: Aft radome and tail navigation and position lights. (All J. Fernandez)*

# Undercarriage

Front view of the nosewheel leg strut and wheel. Note the hydraulic steering unit, to the right. Landing lamp is also visible.

**Inset:** Details of the nosewheel door. (All J. Fernandez)

*Left: Port view of the nosewheel. Wheel hub details are visible.*

*Below: Undercarriage arrangement. Note main undercarriage details.*

*Bottom: Front view of the undercarriage.*

*Opposite page: Main undercarriage details. Note complicated retraction system and hydraulic pipes. Main leg has a reinforcing bracket (silver) which is not an original part of the aircraft. (All J. Fernandez)*

*Three photos of the tail retractable tailwheel/bumper. (All J. Fernandez)*

# Stores

*150 gallon drop tank mounted on inboard pylon. (Richard Dann Collection via J. Fernandez)*

*Total bomb load of the Skyknight was 4,000 lb plus 11 3/4" rockets. 1000lb bomb is shown on the inboard pylon. (Richard Dann Collection via J. Fernandez)*

*Above: Skyknight with AIM-7 Sparrow air-to-air missiles mounted on both pylons. (Richard Dann Collection via J. Fernandez)*
*Below: Preserved AIM-7 Sparrow missile. (J. Fernandez)*